GOD'S GENUINE LOVE
THE *"Root Solution"*
FOR VIOLENCE AND CRIME

Let's Give Him Back *ALL* of His Demonic Tactics!!

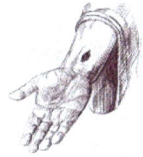 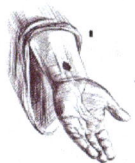

Murder ~ Robbery ~

Theft ~ Crime (Hate Crime) ~ Envy

Jealousy ~ Anger ~ Bitterness

Malice ~ Control of Others ~ Hatred

Temperament~ Weak Minded ~ Violence, etc.

Now, let's love ourselves and every human being on Earth regardless of race or gender.

Copyright © May 2019
Author: Ruby Mack
Proofreader, Editor, & Book Cover Designer: Ruby Mack
Book Cover Publisher: Creative Publishing Book Design

ALL RIGHTS RESERVED

No portion of this publication may be reproduced, stored in any electronic system or transmitted in any form or by any means, electronic, mechanical, photocopy, recording, or otherwise, without written permission from the author. Brief quotations may be used in literary reviews.

Library of Congress Control Number: 2018912317
ISBN: 978-0-578-45665-2

Stop the Violence Book Publishing, LLC
Jackson, MS
Dreamstime images

Disclaimer

This nonfiction book was written to mainly share with the world the "root solution" for violence and crime; God's genuine love and how to incorporate it in your daily living. Also, how to share genuine love and the root solution with our sisters and brothers throughout this world (meaning other nations, countries, etc.).

Exercising the attributes of God's genuine love, which contributes to the "<u>Root Solution</u>" for violence and crime, can positively affect people's behavior. However, this book doesn't guarantee to cease violence and crime in this world, even though I'm confident that it will, and it can also help change people's character, demeanor, and behavior, along with their harsh feelings and temperament reactions toward others in this world.

This awesome, anointed, and life-changing book isn't geared to any specific religion or Christianity, but for <u>all</u> human beings on this earth to unite in love and fulfill your assigned mission given by God. If you have a mental disorder or any other kind of illness whether it's spiritual, physical, or emotional, this book is not a guaranteed cure. You should consult your physician for any psychological problems that you are experiencing.

Acknowledgements

First, I acknowledge the Lord for instilling in my heart from birth—love, compassion and care for the people in this *world*. When I hear of violence and other crimes that are taking place in our society, I feels the victim's pain, also my heart grieves, and it's touched as though my arms are wrapped around those who are bereaved or have been victimized by criminal injustice. However, as a child growing up and being able to understand the criminal activities that are taking place in neighborhoods, communities, schools, etc., I constantly pray to God (from childhood to the present), these words: "Lord, in the name of Jesus, what can I do to *help* the people stop committing crimes and murdering one another, because I'm so tired of grieving and feeling pain in my heart?" Believe it or not, it was in December 2012, when the Lord gave me the shocking answer! With that being said, to reiterate, it's imperative that I acknowledge Almighty God for revealing to my humble spirit and loving heart the answer to my prayer, which is this book to share with the people in this world.

Last, but not least, I would like to acknowledge Mr. Dudley for his awesome and creative input relating to the front book cover design.

Introduction

According to 2016 statistics released by the FBI's annual report, (FBI, This week: 2016 Crime in the United States Report Released) violent crime is on the rise. There were an estimated 17,250 murders in the U.S. last year, an 8.6 percent increase from 2015. Overall, violent crime rose 4.1 percent last year, while property crime fell 1.3 percent compared to 2015 figures. Reports also showed there were an estimated 1.2 million violent crimes in the U.S. last year. Though the violent crime numbers rose from 2015 to 2016, the five-year and 10-year trends show an increase from 2012 (up 2.6 percent). Of the violent crimes reported to police in 2016, aggravated assault made up 64.3 percent, robbery-26.6 percent, rape accounted for 7.7 percent, and murder made up 1.4 percent. In addition, according to the FBI statistical report, there was an estimated 1,197,704 violent crimes committed around the nation, which was an increase from 2014 figures (https://www.fbi.gov).

While listening about all of the violence and crimes that are being committed in this world globally, there's a motive behind it all. We often wonder why children are murdering their parents and vice versa; why are gunmen going on a rampage killing innocent people on their jobs; in their homes; in the schools and in other countries, then turning the gun on themselves. Is it that people are experiencing mental and/or emotional disturbance? Could it be that people don't realize how precious their lives and the lives of others are? Could it be drugs/alcohol controlling their thoughts, minds and behavior? Are people killing others and themselves because they don't know the purpose for their lives? Or, most of all, people just don't know the "genuine love" that God and his son Jesus, have for us.

Most gunmen usually commit suicide after gunning down other innocent people because of the consequences for the crime that was committed. The gunman may also commit suicide because he doesn't want to experience flashbacks of the innocent lives that he has taken. What's it going to take to stop the violence and crime in this world? People are looking for law enforcements, the mayor, president, congress, and other political officials for solutions to the chaos this world is experiencing and in reality, they don't seem to have the appropriate answer. Yes, people in political offices have the power to make laws, pass laws and implement laws, but let's take a look at what the people in this world are doing to make certain laws be established to protect others. For instance, citizens are asking for stricter laws on gun purchasing in which that's a great demand because crime can still be committed with a knife, or another type of weapon instead of a sawed-off rifle, which is mainly used to harm other innocent people. Although guns are needed for protection, the purpose is being reversed to commit crimes and harm other precious and innocent human beings. Needless to say, how can a civilized human being have the heart to harm or kill another individual? Not only harm another being, but unlawfully take what a person has worked hard for in life to possess. Together, we can disband guns and other weapons as a need for protection by allowing your minds to accept *change*; don't allow negative thoughts to incubate in your minds; last but not least, comprehend and implement the beneficial information provided in this life-changing book.

The spirit spoke to me to write on "God's Genuine Love- Stop The Violence", because the world as a whole, which includes the Whitehouse, politicians and other nations, need to know the true meaning of "Genuine Love". It's the knowledge of God's genuine love being instilled in the minds and hearts of all human beings that will have a positive effect on the harsh crimes and violence that are overpowering this world, and it's the knowledge and patterning of God's "genuine love" that can *positively* decrease and cease the murdering and other violence that are sweeping this world rapidly. In addition, *God has genuine love* for all of us and once the world really understands genuine love from its roots, then people can really love themselves and others. Above all, the implementation of God's genuine love along with the *"Root Solution – No Bandages"* Movement, is the answer to violence and crime.

In order for the people in this world learn how to share genuine love, you must first have a heart to *love yourself*, then learn just how much *genuine love* God has for every one of us. However, yes, we as human beings will have disagreements and misunderstandings about some instances, situations, or problems, but the knowledge and implementation about the attributes of "God's genuine love" will help you to seek positive and constructive answers, agreements, and solutions. To reiterate, implementing the attributes of *God's genuine love* can be an avenue to resolve the violence and crime in this world.

Although violence and crime are overwhelming globally, (whites harming whites) and (blacks harming blacks), etc., everyone must be mindful that God has it all in control and we must stay prayerful for his protection. In addition, as a whole, ALL races must understand and accept the fact that all lives matters and were crafted by the only existing and powerful creator. Although Satan is on a rampage, through it all, I have "Good News" — let's start a *New Journey* by mentally programming your minds to willingly accept "Change" in your lives, then learn and implement the **root solution** that is shared in this book to possibly cease violence and crime.

While everybody is anxiously and constantly wondering, watching and waiting for political leaders to find and implement a solution, we must realize that every human being on this earth has the power that's given by God to cease the violence and crime. However, in this book is the **root solution**, so NOW is the time to start implementing it. For centuries the solution for violence and crime has been unsuccessfully discovered and as you can see, incarceration isn't a solution but a bandage. A prime example, in order for an illness, diagnosis, or problem to be cured, you must explore deeper, which is the root and from there start working on a solution and that's exactly what is being shared with you in this book regarding violence and crime and the root solution for both. All you have to do is comprehend what you are reading then immediately start putting it into action.

The bandages (incarceration for one) that are placed on violence and crime along with other problems that affects our daily lives are just a temporary soothing for the problem instead of a **cure**. After the bandages have worn off the problem, we are back to the so-call "drawing board" again, which means political leaders are ignoring the main cause of the problem because they fail to examine the root(s), then plan strategically. Just why political leadership (personnel in higher rank) fail to examine the root of violence and crime the world is experiencing? As you read further into this anointed and inspiring book, which is the root solution for violence and crime—you will also learn more about the *"Root Solution-No More Bandages"* Movement.

TABLE OF CONTENTS

CHAPTER I
Love vs. God's Genuine Love and How He Shares It with Us 1
God's Genuine Love Towards Criminals and Wrong Doers 12

CHAPTER II
Mankind Perception of Love 17
Love in a Relationship 30

CHAPTER III
The Eighteen Attributes of God 37

CHAPTER IV
What Causes Violent Behavior in Humans 43
What Causes Children to be Aggressive/Violent 61
Seven Crimes That Causes Violent Actions 64
Seven Steps to Avoid Domestic Violence in a Relationship 78
How Does God Deal with the Issue of Mass Murder 88

CHAPTER V
What's Your Purpose for Life on Earth 90

CHAPTER VI
Recap: G.G.L.-The Root Solution for Violence & Crime 100
Political Leadership 108
Black Lives Matter 114
The "Root Solution- No More Bandages" Movement 121

CHAPTER VII
Book Summary 125
Author's Page 128

A MESSAGE TO THE WORLD

If my people who are called by my name will humble themselves, pray, seek my face, and turn from their wicked ways, then I will hear from heaven, and will forgive their sins and heal their land.

People, choose TODAY to take heed to what God is saying to us.

II-Chronicles 7:14

CHAPTER ONE
LOVE

VS
GOD'S GENUINE LOVE
AND HOW HE SHARES IT WITH US

We often hear or tell people that we love them, but is it *genuine love* or just a word of mouth? Some people say they love you but will not help you in the time of need. Some people will also say they love you but will scandalize your name; demean and belittle your character; have envy and jealousy towards you; and last but not least, lie on you for no apparent reason. Above all, having knowledge of God's "genuine love" can, without a doubt, have a *positive effect* on the chaos and tragedies this world is experiencing.

Now, let's start from the beginning with *love*. In order for you to really understand the true meaning of love and <u>how</u> to love, you must first understand and embrace it in your heart, mind, and soul just how much God loves us and you must also have a passion to love yourself. Next, let's take a moment to examine some straight forward definitions of the word "love", and from there we will learn about *God's genuine love* in which Jesus, the son of God, is our role model. Alright, "love" — means being attached personally and thought of as having emotional and strong affection. *Another* definition — love is known to be a representation of the kindness that all humans portray or exhibits; their affection and compassionate feelings; their unselfishness, loyalty and benevolent interest for the good of all human beings. *Thirdly*, love is also described as having affection and compassion for all of God's creations which includes humans, animals, and one's self. *Fourth-*

ly, love for all mankind is constituted by being intimate; being caring and having attachment. *Last* but not least, St. Thomas Aquinas stated that his definition for love is having a desire for all mankind to be happy and for another to do well. St. Thomas Aquinas exemplified Christians need to love all mankind, which include those who envy you; those who seek to keep you down; and those who are backstabbers. In other words, you *must* love your enemies. Wow! For some, that's a hard pill to swallow. He also believed that Christianity love is highly motivated by the need to see others succeed in life and to be good people. Love can also be interpersonal, which means involving relationships between people, or, impersonal, meaning human beings' love between themselves or a higher degree of "like". Yes, God gave his only begotten son, "Jesus", to die for us, which is love. Yes, he wakes us up every morning; put shelter over our heads; he's our provider and he blesses us. But, let's learn about that "genuine love" that God and his son have for us and allow the knowledge of this genuine love to dwell in your mind, heart, and inner spirit.

Now that your mind and knowledge regarding some definitions of love have been strengthened, enhanced, or overwhelmed, let's become acquainted with "God's genuine love" and apply it to your daily living. To give you a briefing on genuine love, it's unconditional and unselfishness. Not only that, genuine love includes having extreme patient and gentle kindness; it carries no envy; proudness; boastful; rudeness; hard to anger; self-seeking and unforgiveness; it's rejoiceful with the truth and it has an unacceptable tolerance for evil. *Above all*, genuine love definitely has the best interest for all humans such as perseverance, protection, having strong trust and plenty of hope. (KJV)

As I was growing up, I was taught that God gave his only begotten son to die on the cross so that everybody can have the right to the tree of life. Oh! Yes, that's as genuine (*purified*) as love can get. In addition to that precious sacrifice, God has even more genuine love that he shares with us and that's the Ten Commandments. The Apostle Paul tells his biblical description of love in I-Corinthians, 13:4-8, which states: [4]Love is patient and kind; love is not envious, boastful, arrogant, [5]or rude. It does not insist on its own way; it's not irritable or resentful; [6]It does not rejoice in wrong doing but rejoices in truth. [7]It bears all things, believes all things, hopes all things, and endures all things. [8]Love never ends.

In addition, Apostle Paul shared some powerful scriptures from the Bible pertaining to the awesome love that God has for all mankind and they are: in John 3:16-17, which states: [16]For God so loved the world that he gave his only begotten Son, so that everyone who believes in him may not perish but may have eternal life. [17]Indeed, God didn't send his Son into this world to condemn us, but in order that the world might be saved through him. And again, God's love is exemplified in I-John 4:7-8 and 11-12, which states: [7]Beloved, let us love one another, because love is from God; everyone who loves is born of God and knows God. [8]Whoever doesn't love—doesn't know God, for <u>he is love.</u> [11]Beloved, since God loves us so much, we should also *love one another*. [12] If we love one another, God lives in us, and his love is perfected in us. (KJV)

To sum up all the Godly love scriptures that Apostle John wrote in the Bible, I must add "<u>Genuine</u>" to God's love, not just because of his actions taken for us through his son Jesus, but also the wonderful principles or statues that he set forth for us. Needless-to say, St. Augustine said there's a remarkable difference between love and lust. He explains that an over indulgence is known to be an encounter with lust. St. Augustine also had a relationship with love and he replied, "I was in love with love", which meant he received love in return and he admitted from his experience with love that God's love is *genuine*, because he loves to the fullest, whereas human's love has some complications attached such as, being a victim of envy, anger, jealousy, malice and temperament, just to name several. St. Augustine also stated that God's genuine love offers peace that's not only for him but for *all* mankind.

Now, let's take a tour of God's genuine love for us by being reminded of a set of principles that God created, and two tragic events in the Bible where God's genuine love was shared through forgiveness for committing murder, which is a crime and one of the Ten Commandments. *First,* let's examine the Ten Commandments that God set forth for all human beings to adhere to, which will help instill *genuine love in your heart for yourself and others*. I must say that the Ten Commandments are a set of biblical principles relating to ethics and worship, which play an important critical and fundamental role in our daily lives.

First Commandment:

Thou shall have no other God before me
God is saying to us that we should realize that no human or materialistic object is greater or more valuable than him and he wants us to realize that he's the creator of all humans and objects in this world and nothing should be praised or loved more than him. Yes, God gives us health and strength to work and make money so that we can purchase materialistic items such as a beautiful home, vehicle, jewelry, clothing, etc., that we so desire to make us happy and comfortable, but he doesn't want us to get so tied up and focused on our materialistic assets and forget he's the *provider* who made it all possible for us to possess those items. People also tend to love their companion, pet, or child(ren) more than God, which is being disobedient and not respecting the above commandment.

In comparison, materialistic items and humans can cause violence and crime in the world. For instance, you could be at a store in your fine car and unexpectedly comes an unknown person hijacking you and taking your car. This is an example of the hi-jacker using your car as his God because he feels that your possession is valuable and will satisfy his needs, whether it's just a joy ride, destroy it, or sell your possession for money. However, the Lord is displeased with that criminal act because the criminal has health and strength to work and purchase a vehicle also and receive the same satisfaction. *Choose now to stop the criminal acts*!

Second Commandment:

Thy shall have no other idol before thee
God is saying to be grateful and thankful for the materialistic things that he blesses you with, but more importantly, be thankful for your parents, sibling, relatives, and friends. However, God doesn't want us to worship our valuables nor depend on people for finance or as a god, because he's to be highly glorified, praised, worshipped, trusted and honored at *all* times.

Third Commandment:

Don't Use the Lord's Name in Vain
Using the Lord's name in vain is blaspheming, because his name should be used with respect at *all* times.

Fourth Commandment:

Remember the Sabbath Day and Keep it Holy
For God so <u>loves</u> us until he chose <u>Sunday</u> for us to rest from our labor just as he did, although it's mandatory for some people to work on Sunday. In contrast, people without love in their hearts are always going to and fro seeking to cause harm to others. In fact, they should realize and take in consideration that God worked six days creating good; therefore, they should follow that pattern by working to purchase what they desire instead of robbing and stealing during any day. Honestly, people should attend church and do something constructive that's holy and pleasing to God. Don't commit a crime for it will incarcerate your God-given

precious time and drain your finances of every dime. (a fine)

Fifth Commandment:

Honor your father and mother, that your days may be long upon the land which the Lord your God giveth thee

Your parents are God's genuine love that he shares with you. The Lord is saying that he gives your parents the responsibility and authority to rear and discipline a child according to his will, which is righteous, and parents should be respected and obeyed at *all* times. However, there are parents who spend quality time teaching their child the way God wants him/her to live; all about his righteousness; and how to avoid trouble, but as a child begins to mature, Satan starts manipulating his/her mind and spirit; misleading and pulling the child away from the nature in which he/she was reared. Not only that, Satan starts leading a child his way as the father, which is destructive, demonic, and corrupt— also causing him/her to engage in illegal acts such as drinking, smoking, drugs, violence, committing crimes, etc. People must pray and ask God for *power* and *strength* to overcome Satan's tactics and temptations, while keeping in mind to obey and respect the positive leading and guidance that your parent(s) instilled in you. My God-given mother and father didn't teach me to rob, steal, or kill my fellow sisters and brothers (known and unknown). God will shorten your days upon this earth if you are disobedient and disrespectful to your parent(s).

Six Commandment:

Thou shall not kill (or murder)
People perceive this commandment differently, but I'm relating to it according to God's *genuine love*. He loves us so dearly until he gave his only son to be persecuted and crucified for our sins, healing and salvation. Therefore, why do people in this world go around killing others for whatever reason, whether it's out of an-

ger, robbery, burglary, etc.? Please be reminded that the Lord didn't give nobody the authority to murder your sisters and brothers. Instead, he taught us to love thee one another. Without a doubt, this crime can be avoided by understanding God's genuine love and how he wants you to apply it in your daily living. Needless to say, it's impossible to kill someone you love, and on the other hand, that's not love when another human provokes another individual to kill in self-defense.

People, let's realize that murdering your sisters and brothers isn't biblical because God is the one who gave us life and he didn't give us permission to take any one's life, so let's pattern after God's genuine love and lead the life that God has given us and be happy and content. So, starting today, take control over your mind, thoughts and reactions; henceforth, not allowing the devil to control your behavior. *God gave me life as well as you, let's acknowledge his genuine love and no more murdering in our cities, states, and countries.*

Seventh Commandment:

Thou shall not commit adultery
When a man and woman make a vow to be committed to each other until death do them part, both parties must realize that God created them, and they chose each other to spend eternity until he calls them home (one before the other, or both). However, when both parties are not being honest and faithful to one another and start dating outside their marriage, that can cause violence to arouse. Another instance, if caught with an outside male or female, that can also cause anger to explode and uncontrollable thoughts such as killing, stabbing, or other types of violent injuries travel swiftly through the mind of the companion. Be mindful that if God's genuine love is involved in the relationship, then both parties should have the <u>power</u> to <u>control</u> their minds and bodies from engaging in a sexual relationship outside of their mar-

riage and be satisfied and content with their soul-mate. In return, the outsider should respect the relationship of the man or woman as well.

Eighth Commandment:

Thou shall not steal
God's genuine love states that whatever we ask in his name we shall receive it. Yes, that's genuine love because God doesn't put any stipulations or limitations on our asking. He doesn't want us stealing from family members, out of stores, from neighbors and other people because that's ungodly to steal people's possessions that they've inherited. Not only that, there's no genuine love in one's heart to hurt another person's heart and emotions by stealing their belongings. However, stealing can cause violence and that's what we are trying to *avoid* by patterning after God's *genuine* love, because he makes a way for you to get what you want without stealing it. In addition, people must remember that when asking God for what you want be specific, patient and faithful, for he will present it at a suitable time. Also, when asking God for what you want, he may not present it to you the way you had planned to receive it, because he has supernatural ways to fulfill your needs and desires. For instance, he may allow a person to bless you with it; he may lead you to a store that has an affordable price; he may bless you with a job; an unexpected increase or even overtime so that you can afford to buy what you desire. Remember, thou shall not steal; just pray and ask God for what you want—believe and at his appointed time you will receive, just to reiterate.

I worked for mines and got it through God's will — ask the Lord for yours; keep the faith and patience — Please Don't Steal.

Ninth Commandment:

Thou shall not bear false witness against your neighbor

Bearing false witness means lying and "neighbor", means mankind — not only the lovely person who lives next to you or maybe in your neighborhood. Violence erupts when people lie on others to someone else regardless of the situation — whether it's relationship related, marriage, conversational, or "he say", "she say". The *tongue* can be used as a *deadly weapon* causing someone to kill or injure other human beings. What you witness about someone else shouldn't be shared if it's going to cause violence and on the other hand, you shouldn't make matters worse by bearing false witness (lying about what you actually witnessed).

In today's world, you would be amazed and astounded about the numerous criminal acts that are being committed such as murder, assault, and other injuries due to people bearing false witness. Reiterate words, "he say", "she say". To illustrate, there may have been a couple who were married for numerous years and perhaps the female would happen to be a school teacher. Well, the husband may receive word from a neighbor or someone who is jealous of their relationship, so that person tells the husband that his wife has been seeing another male. Instead of the husband waits until the wife comes home to confront her about the "she say" (lying and bearing false witness), the husband gets angry and decides to visit the school where his wife works and kills her in front of her class and the wife had no idea of the motive. Later, the husband finds out that the rumor wasn't true, but an innocent life has been taken. I must say that people who bear false witness must answer to God. In addition, people in this world should take the first six months to sweep around their own front door (mind their own business), and the next six months to leave other people's business alone (whether it's telling the truth or bearing false witness). For God's genuine love teaches us to be humble, meek, and kind.

Tenth Commandment:

Thou shall not covet thy neighbor's house

God is saying that you should not be envious or jealous of other people including your neighbor. He's not only speaking of a physical house but people's life style; their positive spirits; their personality; their attractiveness and their possessions. This is one commandment people don't adhere to, which causes a substantial amount of criminal altercations. To illustrate, there may be someone who purchased a nice home and a beautiful car, and the Lord also blessed them with a good paying job to fulfill their heart's desires. In contrast, another person who may not even know that person who's living and riding nice but envy him/her, so the bad guy decides to break in that person's house to destroy and steal his/her belongings and car, then take it somewhere to wreck or strip it. I must warn you, that is not God's genuine love and I'm advocating to obey this commandment and stop the criminal acts.

Some very incredible and awesome principles that illustrate God's genuine love for all mankind have been shared with you thus far, so as you continue to read, I want you to allow this genuineness to dwell in your spirit, mind, and heart. Allow all negative thoughts or feelings that you have within toward any human being(s) in this world to diminish. Now, we are on our way to becoming genuine (pure/real) and exercising that genuinely love for one another. As you continue to read and learn about genuine love, start incorporating it in your daily living towards all humankind. To strengthen or enhance your belief and knowledge about God's "genuine" love, familiarize yourself with the following biblical verses: **John 3**:16; **I-John 4**:7-12; and **Matthew 5**:43-48.

Abiding by the Ten Commandments will result in true spiritual, mental, emotional, and physical guidance for your life. On the other hand, killing, lying, stealing, and adultery are harmful to your immune system. Needless to say, there are consequences written in the Bible regarding violence and committing a crime, which are known to be evil. I highly encourage you to take the time to <u>read</u> every topic and verse(s) shared with you on the following page, so that you will be able to distinguish between love (which is of God), and evil, (which is of Satan).

-TOPICS-

1) Evil in a man's heart (Job 31: 9-12)

2) Evil heart (James 1:13-15)

3) Price paid for evil lifestyle (Hosea 4:10)

4) Negative view of life's meaning (Job 14:1-2)

5) Good, evil lifestyles (Proverbs 4:18-19)

6) God will punish evil doers (Zachariah 5:1-4)

7) Judgment of God upon evil (Revelation 16: 5-7)

8) Massive Act of Revenge (Judges 20: 1-48)

9) Pre-Meditated Murder (Genesis 27: 41-45)

10) Hired Murderer (Deuteronomy 27:25)

11) Killing in Self-defense (II-Samuel 2:22-23)

12) Jealousy – the cause of murder (I-John 3:12)

13) Practicing Deceit (Psalms 101:7)

14) Hurting Another Brings Greater Hurt to Self (Jerem. 7:18-19)

15) Attitude of Mind Dictates Lifestyle (Philippians 4:8-9)

16) Insubordination unwilling to do evil (I-Sam. 22:16-17)

GOD'S GENUINE LOVE TOWARDS CRIMINALS AND WRONG DOERS

To reiterate, God's love is pure, and he does forgive us for any crime or wrong doing that we might engage in, only if we sincerely ask for forgiveness and repent. Not only that, God pre-paid the price for all human beings' sins by allowing his son to suffer, die, and hang on the cross. All mankind must not take God's love, grace and mercy for granted by committing crimes and wrong doings just because he <u>graciously</u> forgives. As we all know, Satan does exist, and he goes to and fro seeking weak-minded people who have *no control over their thinking, temper, and actions*. Those are the personal traits that Satan preys on and uses his wicked power to force humans to become victims of wrong doing and engage in criminal activities. On the other hand, people must be mindful that a pure and loving spirit speaks positive words and action into one's spirit and mind. Anything that lives in the mind, heart or thoughts that are negative, violent or harmful, is the trick of Satan targeting you as a member of his satanic workshop. Nevertheless, when that unpleasant voice speaks to your mind and spirit, rebuke it in the name of "Jesus" and always stay focused on God's genuine love and the <u>positive action</u> and <u>affection</u> that he commands all mankind to show towards one another.

People often wonder if they are disobeying God's commandments by defending themselves or their property from criminals. In my *opinion*, a person isn't disobeying any of the commandments that God established for us to adhere to in our lives. For instance, if an intruder enters your home to afflict harm upon you and take your possessions—without a doubt, you have the right to protect yourself and your assets, for the intruder will have to answer to God and the victim just need to ask God for forgiveness for the action taken to defend him/herself. Another example in which God's genuine love forgives—if you're in a situation where you're hi-jacked; your purse snatched; or you catch a thief in action breaking in your vehicle—God gives us five senses and he won't punish us for defending what he blessed us with whether it's tangible or intangible. (*Take precaution of the legal consequences as well*). With that being said, the *purpose* of this book is to share God's genuine love and to instill that same love in every human's mind and heart, so that no one will become a victim of crime and have to retaliate defensively. In return—no one will be labeled as a criminal.

Let's stop the violence and criminal activities and love ye one another just as God loves. Next, to verify that God will forgive criminals, there are two biblical events that will justify my claim for forgiveness and the first one is when Pharaoh had newborn males killed. Pharaoh was concerned about the Egyptian Empire where the Israelites flourished in Egypt and he didn't want to eject them from Egypt because they were too valuable, so he sought to control their numbers by forced labor and by child slaughter. Pharoah told the midwives that every male baby must be killed as soon as they were born. This plan was thwarted by the Hebrew midwives, including Shiphrah and Puah, so Pharaoh ordered instead, that every newborn Israelite boy be hurled into the Nile waters and left to drown. Over the years, this must have happened to many thousands of newborn Israelite boys. (Exodus I:15-22). (http://www.womeninthebible.net/bible)

Pharaoh was also a man with no heart and used his authority to demand others to kill innocent newborn males. As you can see, Pharaoh was held accountable for his evil, hateful, and disastrous actions. On the other hand, do you think the Lord forgave him for his criminal behavior by ordering children to be killed as soon as they enter the world and not allowing them to fulfill the mission for their lives? Yes, if mean old Pharaoh repented, although he still may have received discipline from the Lord. Lastly, in spite of what crime a person may have committed, just repent sincerely from the heart and you will be forgiven because the Lord mercifully allows an opportunity to use you for his kingdom.

The second tragic biblical event is when Jehu slaughters the royal children. Jehu was an army captain who led a coup d'état against the royal house of Israel and he killed Jehoram who was the brother of Ahaziah. Jehu had Jezebel's body (a powerful queen of Israel) thrown out of the window of her palace, and then trampled to death by chariot horses driven over her still-living body. Jehu, a merciless and cold-hearted army captain, had no remorse for what he ordered to be done to Jezebel. After the murder was carried out as he ordered, he went and ate dinner. The remains of Jezebel were her skull, feet and the palms of her hands, which were left to be buried because the dogs had eaten her flesh. Read (II-Kings 9:31-37) (http://www.womeninthebible.net/)

Not only was Jehu accessory to murder because he ordered Jezebel to be thrown out the window of her palace, but he actually committed a mass murder by rounding up all of the family, friends and supporters of the royal family and slaughtered them. Male children were included in this mass murder since they would one day grow up and perhaps seek revenge. Of course, Jehu provided assistance with slaughtering innocent people. The boys' heads were hacked off, collected in baskets, and displayed for a gawky crowd at the city gate. (https: www.womeninthebible.net) As you can see, there were people in the Bible who were also hard-hearted, evil, hateful, and gruesome just like some individuals are today. Do you think that Jehu probably had no knowledge of love, or didn't believe in God's genuine love through his son Jesus Christ? Just like God forgave Jehu for his wrong doing, *if he repented*, he will forgive a murderer provided that he/she is sincere when seeking forgiveness. There's still hope for murderers in the eyesight of God, just be sincere when forgiveness is asked for from the father through his son Jesus. (*That doesn't mean to take advantage of God's mercy by killing people because he's the one to decide when and exactly how the criminal will receive disciplinary action*). I'm justifying that a murderer can be cleansed with the powerful blood of Jesus; receive salvation; become a warrior for the Lord and last but not least, he can also gain knowledge about the "root solution" and join the *"Root Solution – No More Bandages"* Movement. When you become a supporter for "The Root Solution Movement" (ceasing violence and crime), that means you are sharing compassion and putting forth effort in this world to cease violence and crime, whether it's in your community, neighborhood, school, etc., to implement "God's Genuine Love-the Root Solution for Violence and Crime", which is the <u>answer</u> and not a *bandage* to the violence and crime that are spreading all over the world like a cancer. In addition, if you have been a criminal or a victim of a crime, this will be a great opportunity to testify to others and warned them of the effects that violence and crime have on your health, emotions, character, reputation and soul.

To reiterate, I'm not justifying that *not adhering* to the Ten Commandments is the right thing to do. Instead, I'm informing those who have broken one or more of the Ten Commandments, there's still hope and you don't have to allow your mistake to become cancerous because if God forgave back in the biblical days, most definitely he's in the forgiveness business <u>right today</u>, and you can resume living a normal, prosperous and successful life by fulfilling the ordained, appointed purpose for your valuable life and be happy while you travel your spiritual and physical journey and don't be bound and shackled to condemnation. Never allow anyone to keep you in bondage by constantly reminding you of your past; setting guidelines for you to abide by; or tells you there's no hope for your situation because of your sins. Just know they are Satan's elves trying to lead you into destruction or force you to become violent and commit a crime. Another bondage people often experience is mental or emotional. To loose those shackles as well, just ask the Lord for strength and deliverance while maintaining a positive focus and never yielding or dwelling on negative or evil thoughts. Yes, continue to comprehend what you are reading because you can be set free to fulfill your purpose for life on this earth.

People, I must inform you that no one can live your life nor think for you. You must be in total control at all times and use your brains that the Lord gave you to make right decisions and be mindful that the Lord is your leader and his will for your life is to be free and not live in bondage and condemnation because he's the only judge and ruler over all. Nevertheless, have you ever been told that what you are experiencing in life is a curse or the Lord is paying you back because you didn't help someone, mainly a relative or close friend? You know that's the first thing people in general will say especially if you don't allow them to use you and walk on you as a dependent rug and drain you dry of your kindness and love. Yes, people will really feel that you're being punished because you turned them down for whatever reason. Of course, if you are in Christ, some people will really try to take advantage of your loving kindness, and if you don't allow it, they will judge you as a hypocrite but don't fall for that satanic manipulation—when you know the relationship that you have with the Father, don't let Satan elves belittle you and your blessed values. In addition, have you ever met someone who claims to have the answer to everything that you're experiencing in life? Have you ever been told by others that you'll never be delivered from the wrong that you are doing or have done because your parents did the same so it's genetic (or in your family line genes)? Have you ever told maybe a friend or relative your desires or dreams for your life and you received a negative response or opinion such as, "Oh! No, I can't see you doing that because of something you probably have done wrong in the past? Just know that if a person can't give you constructive opinions, answers, or words of encouragement, that individual is trying to keep you in bondage and condemnation and possibly keep you on his/her level or try to keep you from progressing, reaching your goals, fulfilling your dreams and the mission the Lord has assigned to your precious and valuable life. It's fine to talk or ask opinions about something you don't quite understand, but never allow people's opinion or answer lead your life because our Father has the answer for it all.

CHAPTER II

MANKIND PERCEPTION OF LOVE

Speaking of interpersonal love, which means an experience felt by a person for another person; and identifying or caring for a person or thing. Although you might not know it, love is known to be an activity and action such as giving, sharing, and doing. However, from a human's perspective of love, it can be interpreted in many areas such as emotional, spiritual, etc. Nevertheless, sometimes a person may often say that you should only love those who deserve it or earned it and sometimes they are speaking of exactly what a person has done for them or has given them which is, in my opinion, showing care, a portion of love, and not the full capacity of love or genuine love.

People often view love as showing affection, such as sharing a hug or kiss. Also, love is often perceived by someone when another person, whether it's a relative, friend or stranger, gives you tangible items such as money, gifts, a car, etc. Although the perception of "love" is a very broad word that can be discussed or elaborated on in many different formalities, I would like to remind you that "love" can't be *purchased*. In short terms, you can't make nobody love you regardless of what you do for them; what you buy them; even if you are by their side during their storm, or while they are experiencing tests, trials/or tribulations (hard trying times, per say). No doubt, it will still be something missing in people's lives that they will expect you to fulfill and if you failed to do so, they will feel unloved — not thinking about all that <u>you have done</u> and what <u>you have given</u> tangibly or intangibly.

My perspective of love is being able to love those whom you see and those whom you don't see; those whom you know and don't know. When I speak of love, I'm speaking of having feelings, compassion, concern, consideration, caring, sympathy, empathy, a heart and respect for everybody meaning <u>all</u> races, gender, origin, nationality, and geographic. I also view love as being able to pray for people whom you know and those whom you don't know (that's having a heart and being concerned and compassionate); asking God to save them; heal them; bless them, protect them, and give them their heart's desire, if it's within God's will. In addition, love isn't always *materialistic*. When I tell someone that I love them whether they're relatives, church members; people I meet in public places; or classmates — I'm saying that it was a pleasure to see them, meet them, to know them, that I'm praying for them and if my assistance is ever needed, I'm there for them. On the other hand, love goes deeper when it comes to my own flesh and blood, (which are my children). In contrast, I have always and still tell them, "I love you", as well as shown and constantly show my love for my children regardless of their age, because "love" should be like marriage, and that is until death do you part (in the physical realm), and love should also remain in your heart when you are separated due to death. Although I always have been a single parent who fulfilled two marvelous and awesome roles of a mother and father, I have always shown and shared love with my children from the newborn stage up to adulthood, by teaching them the principles of life; how to love and respect everybody (not just elders); the fundamentals of education (such as learning how to count; the alphabets; how to pronounce and spell their name; their birthdate; how to say "yes sir" and "yes mam", etc.). My children were also taught how to be well-groomed; how to love and care for their mate; house chores such as how to wash dishes; clean and mop; how to cook. But most importantly, how to pray and the importance of being reared in church learning all about the Lord; what he expects from us and most importantly, what is our mission. _Proverbs 22:6_ says, "If you train a child up in the way he should go; and when he is old, he will not depart from it." Although the Bible states "He", this verse is speaking to females as well, and I can attest to that biblical verse, for it does fit well in a family relationship.

In addition, my love is so strong and compassionate for the people in this world until it seems as if everyone has a place in my humble heart—those whom I know and those whom I'm not associated with. Illustration, when I hear about tragedies, homicides, and people suffering with an illness such as cancer, heart attacks, strokes, diabetes, etc., I begin to feel a pain within my heart and a spirit of grief begins to over shower me, and I often find tears streaming from my eyes as I begin to cry out to the Lord on the behalf of the one who is victimized. I also find myself including them in my prayers daily asking the Lord what can I do to help the people in this world to stop committing crimes, killing, robbing, etc., and help them to love one another, because I'm tired of my heart feeling pain for the one who commits a crime and the innocent victims who experience a painful and tragic effect due to violence?" Well, the Lord didn't answer me immediately—years passed. Finally, in December 2012, while standing in the mirror combing my hair, a voice spoke to me as if it was in the room with me and said to write a book and title it "God's Genuine Love—Stop The Violence." Shockingly! I said, "Oh! No. Lord, I love to proof and edit." Nevertheless, I wasn't disobedient so quickly, I found a pen and paper and started listening to the still, sweet voice for additional instructions. Without a doubt, my obedience to write this book is going to have a positive effect in this world including our government officials (president, governor, congress, etc.).

The Bible states that we must love our neighbors and enemies. However, neighbors not only mean those who live next to you or near you, but people in other cities, states, countries, creed, nationality, race, (the entire world). To love them don't mean you must like or approve of their *negative*, unethical actions. However, to have genuine love for someone requires knowing the genuine love God shares with us. In addition, real love is also considered an "action", such as sharing positive thoughts with other people as a whole. The Bible refers to love as a "surpassing way," and as something that's pursued". (*I-Corinth. 12:31* and *14:1*). Nevertheless, the true love of God impels us to do what is pleasing to him and to uphold his sovereignty. Not only that, it moves us to avoid loving the world and its ungodly ways. (*I-John 2:15-16*). Another scripture—those who *love* God hate what's bad (*Psalms 97:10*). The love of God requires us to listen to his voice and be obedient at all times. The Bible says the love of God means that we observe his commandments (*I-John 5:3*). Another *loving* scripture is: *I-John 3:18*—let's love, neither in word nor with the tongue, but indeed and truth. I deeply feel and believe that to love and care for others, you must first love and care for yourself. To illustrate, if you love yourself so dearly, under no circumstance will you provoke any kind of harm or affliction upon yourself and you will have the same feelings toward others. In contrast, if you don't love or care for yourself and is willing to put your life in jeopardy by committing a crime or indulging in violence, quite naturally those characteristics or feelings will be displayed towards another human being in some form of violence or crime.

According to Philosopher Julian Baggini, "love is a kind and passionate commitment that will nurture and develop, even though it usually arrives in our lives unbidden." That's why it's more than just a powerful feeling and without commitment, it's mere infatuation; without passion, it's mere dedication and without nurturing, even the best can wither and die. In addition, love is known to be a driver for positive events. Not only that, but love is also known to be less defined and easily experienced. Indeed, love is one thing that shouldn't ever hurt anyone. (Phil. Julian B.)

Although genuine (true) love consists of many components, I would like to share several of them with you. Please don't just read them but comprehend and allow this valuable information to rest in your heart, mind, and digestive system, then begin to utilize genuine love in your family relationship, (marriage, dating, etc.). Now, the *first* component of true (genuine) love speaking of an intimate relationship is <u>attractiveness.</u> When two people are attracted to each other, the chemistry clings to each other just like a magnet clings tightly to metal and the bonding of the attraction could possibly lead to a romantic desire. However, if only one individual has that feeling, then the relationship could be a wild bizarre fantasy. The *second* known component is intimacy, which plays a major and important role in all relationships such as family, marriage, dating, etc. To get to know and feel very comfortable with each other and revealing yourself such as your true character, behavior, etc. — can help form a strong and true emotional bonding, which will draw you two closer and over a period of time, there's a possibility that the relationship will begin to escalate. The *third* component is <u>attachment.</u> When starting a relationship, first you must be attracted to each other in order to become attached. However, being attached means there's a possibility that the love for each other can be short-term or long-term. Although people differ in a relationship, the term of it — whether it's several years or several months, can transform into something beautiful such a shacking and/or romantic relationship. Needless to say, sometimes that bonding and attachment transform sooner than the couple expects it. With certainty, after revealing yourself to each other and spending quality time throughout the years, both partners can attest that they are comfortable with each other and together have experienced some of life's difficulties. Now both partners can say that the bonding and attractiveness remain the same or perhaps, have gotten stronger and marriage is possible.

Fourth, is <u>commitment</u>, which is a strong and crucial component of true love. A genuine love relationship requires both partners to be committed to one another which means exercising caring and is there for each other through thick and thin (during good and bad times; hard times and sad times, etc.). *Last*, but not least, along with the previously mentioned components is <u>friendship</u>, which makes up a dynamic illustration of true love. Next, allow me to share with you what *true love* **isn't**, although people have a tendency to use the four-letter word to *manipulate* others such as their family members, companion, friends, and most importantly, the church congregation, yes! *First*, is the term "manipulation", which isn't a positive tool for sharing genuine love and just know that "love" is a marvelous gift from God and it <u>shouldn't</u> be used as a tool to <u>control</u> people's feelings and emotions by forcing them or convincing them to prove their love by engaging in something against their own will. For example, telling your companion or spouse, "If you love me then you would by me a Mercedes or maybe a mink coat." What if the companion isn't financially able? So, instead of accepting the financial shortage, you convince the companion to show love even if the mate has to borrow, steal, or whatever means needed to satisfy your infatuated desire. *Secondly,* **love isn't** true and genuine if someone ask you, or perhaps, try to force you to engage in an act or speak in a so-called "foreign language", also known as profanity, which is not your nature. On the other hand, becoming <u>passionately violent</u> with someone whom you dearly love, whether it's your parent, sibling, friend, or soul-mate isn't true or genuine love. Yes, sometimes your love one can spark flames through disagreements, misunderstandings, etc., but *emotional* or *physical* violence isn't genuine love.

I would like to share my input and prayerfully translate some people's thoughts, feelings, understanding, and mentality about the phrase, "love leads to giving", and "giving leads to love." First of all, people must understand and realize that whether we are speaking of intimate, physical, or spiritual love, you can't buy it with *money, assets, fortune, or fame*. Now, speaking of intimate love, some people fall in love at first sight. However, that can definitely be a scamming line used to get what a person wants from another individual. On the other hand, falling in love at first can be a possibility. Perhaps, the man laid his eyes on a female that he saw for the first time and happens to see some qualities or values in her that might be common to his or maybe "turns him on." Not only that, the male probably has in his mind the kind of personality or traits that he would like to have in a friend or companion. There's also a possibility that he had been praying for a special kind of woman and was in the right place at the right time to see and meet her. Consequently, speaking of emotional or physical love, when I meet a male, I do not fall in love at first sight—it's imperative that I get to know him better such as his personality, attitude, character, along with his likes and dislikes and from there, to make a long story short and sweet, my like or interest in him could transform to intimate love over a period of time but it's not promising.

Now, let's elaborate on "giving leads to love." I can really write a book on the different aspects of love, but let's talk about an area where this phrase is highly misconstrued, and people being brain-washed and manipulated in churches. Giving, as most pastors see it, shouldn't always be in the form of money. People can give their hearts to God; receive salvation, give up their sins, etc., as a form of love. People shouldn't *always* have to give additional monies because the pastor asks for it. In turn for love, people can volunteer some of their service to the church. Perhaps, people in various churches and denominations think and strongly believe that giving all of their earnings, in addition to their tithes and offerings, is showing love to God through the pastor who is the overseer of all monies collected whether it's through the *mail, congregational giving, product sales*, etc. Numerous people have approached me asking my *opinion* on several reactions they observed by some people in various churches and why they even place money on the platform while the pastor is delivering the Sunday speech instead of attesting to what they agree with by saying Amen. Those questionable people also wondered if it could be because exactly something that is justifiable to their situation or lifestyle has been spoken. They also stated that sometimes in various churches the pastor may even ask for additional money just because the pastor knows the congregation will freely give. Well, if that is happening in the churches, in my opinion, that's *manipulation* and *taking advantage* of God's handmaidens and in his eyesight that is unjust, untruthful and disloyal as a spiritual leader and the pastor will be held an accountable for his/her unjust and unethical behavior.

"Giving leads to love" — in the churches today, the pastors should love people because they took a step to enter into the house of the Lord. Perhaps, some of them are already saved, while others are coming to receive salvation, which means people are giving their hearts and lives to God and the pastors should love that because it's their responsibility to bring souls into the kingdom and that heaven has been bought for us with a price and not money when the Lord gave his only begotten son to die on the cross so that we might have the right to the tree of life. Just know that we all have an eternal home when we leave this world, and it's our choice of either Heaven (which is already paid in full), or Hell — in which you cannot buy an exit out with money or assets. Now, you know that your giving (tithes — 10%, and offerings — no specified amount stated in the Bible), and **not all** of your earnings, should have love for you in the pastor's heart. And in return, pastors should show their love for members and others in the time of need — on special occasions such as birthdays and holidays, instead of asking for all of the congregation's earnings to be deposited into their personal bank account (only using the church expenses to drain the people). A pastor's love should also be given because of your obedience to give in tithe and offering according to the Bible. In addition, pastors should show some love and care for people, especially their members when they are in a crisis, and shouldn't have a *clique* or *special ones* to assist maybe because they give exceedingly more than others, or for any other apparent reason(s). *Pastors,* be like God — give love in return and have no respecter of person to extend your assistance to, which is showing care and sharing *genuine* love.

Another ungodly situation that has been misconstrued, hypnotized, brainwashed, and manipulated in the churches toward God's humble-hearted, handmaidens related to giving is the church's budget. What the church congregation fail to realize and also should keep in mind when it comes to giving <u>all</u> of your money to the pastor (which they use the church expenses and seed-sowing as an alibi) — don't get so hypnotized and mesmerized in a manipulating and entertaining speech until you start *reacting before you think*. People should be mindful that some pastors will pretend to love you and allow you a position in the church or *clique* only because of all your earnings you have deposited or is able to give. Yet, that's not the love of God — it's <u>pretense</u> love from the flesh. I was also informed by another group of people in Christ that in some churches people get so hypnotized and mesmerized about "a word" from the pastor that seems to be plagiarized from another pastor's sermon, until they just start releasing their <u>bill money</u> or residual funds to the platform. Well, I must say that yes, pastors who are deceitful, greed, conning, scamming, and using the Lord's name to <u>gain wealth</u> by misleading the people in the church will give an account for taking advantage of the phrase "giving leads to love." In contrast, "genuine love" is what every pastor that is *"called and ordained"* by God, should give to the people by preaching the <u>truth</u> and not money, entertaining, and manipulative messages. (Information that's pleasing to the people ears, hearts, minds, and daily living).

As I mentioned earlier, be advised and knowledgeable that every church has, or should have a budget in place for the operation of God's house. Most people who attend church are not familiar with a budget but, in short, what it consists of is all the expenses to operate the church such as (staff payroll, utility bills, estimated repairs, unforeseen crisis, and monies set aside to help the needy). Needless to say, that's where your tithes and offerings are to be deposited to maintain that specific amount in the budget. When a pastor preaches on additional giving and perhaps, might manipulate you by saying the Lord is going to do this or that for you, or bring a seed to plant for your breakthrough or your healing; or for whatever conning reason the pastor chooses to bait you with, don't fall for that—just know that you already have a blessing coming just for giving a love offering and your tithes. On the other hand, if you should decide to participate, pray quickly and get the approval from God. I can really write a book on this phrase about *"giving leads to love"* in the spiritual realm, but I'm closing with what I have just shared with you and I pray that you will not allow animosity to breathe in your humble and kind spirits towards me and just know that my love for you is genuine and it will hurt and dampen my heart to hear of, or even if I saw humbled, kind-hearted, God-loving people being robbed, brainwashed, manipulated and misled about the words "love" and "giving", in any church. Pastors should give what they are always asking for sometimes (money), to show their love and care as well, instead of always being a hypnotic, manipulating vacuum cleaner that's always wanting to slurp up additional monies all because they know that loving, and kind-hearted people are going to be obedient to their pastor's request and surrender their funds. People in the house of the Lord, think and pray before you do and take heed to the true meaning of love and "genuine love".

Here's what the Lord says about *sowing a seed and reaping a harvest*—hopefully this will also help you to understand the biblical way of *additional giving*. You can be in control of your own destiny and the wealthy reaper of your own harvest and the seeds that are sown are your key to the harvest. Nevertheless, God has placed certain seeds in your life, some physical, others spiritual, mental, and financial and not only is it important in knowing <u>when</u> to sow your seeds but also <u>where</u> to sow them. Perhaps, a kind word spoken at the right time is a good reaping seed. However, money matters, giving and tithing into ministries that are *really performing* a positive, honest and true work for God is sowing <u>good seeds</u>. Ephesians 6:8 says: "Whatever good thing I make happen for someone else, God will make happen for me." When sowing a seed, God is not looking at the amount you give but your attitude, for he loves a cheerful giver. Be knowledgeable about the principle of sowing and reaping which applies to every area of your life, not just your finances as some pastors always speak about when talking about sowing seeds for your harvest.

The Bible states, "Whatsoever a man soweth, that shall he also reap." For instance, if you sow a *bad seed*, you will reap a bad seed (Galatians 6:7), and whatever you deposit is going to be returned to you. For instance, if you demean someone's character, then at some point in life someone will demean your character. Another example, if you smile in someone's face, while stabbing them in the back, you will, without a doubt experience the same, so just be genuine and real and not a "snake" in the grass. Please familiarize yourself with the given scriptures of sowing and reaping so that you will not be misled about the various ways to sow in addition to your tithes and offerings. For instance: a) sow tears—reap joy (Psalms 126.5); sow righteousness—reap reward (Proverbs 11:18); sow injustice—reap calamity (Proverbs 22:8).

What is true giving? Normally, when you speak of the word "giving", people often think of something materialistic or tangible, such as money, clothes, food or maybe a ride to a specific place. However, I would like to share with you the meaning of "true giving". *First of all*, true giving must consist of care and having compassion for the receiver, whether you know that person or not. *Secondly*, true giving is when you help someone from the heart and not brag or boast about it. Instead, thank the Lord that you were able to offer help to fulfill a need. *Thirdly*, in order to truly give, you are respecting the person's inability to fulfill the need on his or her own. *Fourthly*, by truly giving to a recipient, there's a possibility that you are helping that person to avoid a crime or prevent violence. In contrast, just be cautious of those who pretend to be helpless or homeless and are out on the streets holding up signs and wearing dirty clothes wanting you to be sympathetic for them even though they have a banking account, nice ride and living descent. Those people are of Satan trying to block the assistance for those who are really helpless, homeless and has a disability. Beware of them! Those are not the individuals that the Lord wants you to truly give and bless.

<u>Opening Yourself to Others.</u> The effect of genuine and other oriented giving is profound. It allows you into another person's world and opens you up to perceiving his or her goodness. At the same time, it means investing part of yourself in others, enabling you to love this person as you love yourself. The more love you give, the more you love. This is why your parents (who've given you more than you'll ever know); undoubtedly, love you more than you love them, and you in turn, will love your own children more than they'll love you because deep intimate love emanates from knowledge of giving, it comes not overnight but over time (http://www.aish.com). Speaking of opening yourself to others, doesn't mean you have to provide or kindly give to everybody that asks for a financial favor or a good deed. In addition, opening yourself to others doesn't mean you have to tell people all of your business and accept their opinions. On the other hand, being open means to allow others to get to know you by being friendly, respectful and courteous. Be a great role model so that others will want to follow in your shoes. Learn about and set an example of God's genuine love towards other people. Allow me to briefly discuss opening yourself in two different areas and they are: 1) In a romantic or marital relationship and 2) with others such as friends, family, pastor, co-workers, etc. *First, in* a romantic relationship, opening yourself with your partner means being honest and truthful about the topic being discussed. Of course, neither of you will admit if you have been tipping around, but if the both of you would be honest about what your likes and dislikes are, that's a possibility of avoiding violence and misunderstandings. *Secondly*, opening up to friends means to understand each other

and share your views and understanding about whatever it is that you all feel free to talk about. For heaven's sake don't get deep into what's going on in your personal life because sometimes friend(s), family member(s), pastor, co-worker whom you thought was really trustworthy and would keep your information confidential, will be the main ones (sometimes) to use your situation to blackmail or condemn you. On the other hand, there are some people in this world that you can really trust and open yourself up to and the main ones should be your parents. It is a great privilege when you have someone whom you can be open with because it is like venting in which some people vent a certain problem within and sometimes that isn't good because the problem or thought can escalate into something more serious, but when you have that someone whom you can be opened with and vent, that could save you from violence or crime and maybe from traveling the wrong road in life, so just like any other topic or concern, opening yourselves to others has its pros and cons so you have to be careful and cautious to whom you open yourself up with or to. If you would take the time to listen to the still voice of Jesus, you will never go wrong because he will speak and let you know who you can trust with certain information or concerns you may have because he does use certain people to speak for him a blessing into your life or gives them answers to what you are thinking within and afraid to share it with others due to trust.

I have had problems opening up to others and discussing what I'm feeling deep within because it never failed, when the one I thought I could open up to, gets mad with me then use what I discussed with them against me to try and hurt or belittle me, which is very painful emotionally. Above all, just know that King Jesus is always available to listen, so open yourself up to him because he knows what you're thinking before you even think it and he knows exactly what you're experiencing in life and he's just waiting for you to open up and allow him to give you directions and answers to whatever you're holding or thinking within.

LOVE IN A RELATIONSHIP

In a relationship, love is comprised of emotional, physical, spiritual and mental components, whether you know it or not. When two people commit themselves to each other, they have agreed to love each other in all four ways previously mentioned. However, love in a relationship shouldn't be about <u>only</u> what can you do for each other but being there for each other at all times (the good, bad, sick times, hard times, during bereavement, financially, etc.). In some relationships, the word, "love", is hardly told to one or the other, and you would really be amazed of how the togetherness and feelings would grow in the relationship if that was seriously told to each other more often. In contrast, the word "love", may be verbally stated to one or the other in a relationship, but it's hardly shown. On the other hand, love is rather shown than told, but it would make a big difference in the relationship if one another would tell each other "I love you", and meant it from deep within, and not because of what is done in the physical realm such as serenading with materialistic valuables or some dead presidents (money). No, I'm not saying gifts and materialistic items are not a physical mean of showing love—I'm saying will you continue to love each other when materialistic items can't longer be presented or given? If you said *yes,* your love will still remain the same in your relationship, then you have genuine love because God still loves us when we experience crisis and even when we sin. Nevertheless, regardless of what we experience, God is immutable (same yesterday, today and forever, and his character, grace, and mercy for us will never change).

In order to have "genuine" (real, true, and pure) love in a loving relationship, without hesitation, welcome the Lord in as the head; learn to communicate with each other effectively; have a complete understanding; last, but not least, care and cater to each other. For example, it's not the female's job to be a custodian, maid, waitress, or slave—it's both mates' responsibility to keep the dwelling clean; responsibility to cook (if both individuals know how to cook); responsibility to pay bills, etc. Of course, it's understandable if only one individual in the household is working, then more household responsibilities would fall on the one who is unemployed. Nevertheless, one must realize that house chores are actually a tiresome and boring job within itself. Yes! Believe it or not, it's labor that requires strength and time, so the *working individual* shouldn't take the unemployed mate for granted but be appreciative that he/she is still laboring for the household. However, there's a difference when the unemployed is taking the employed mate for granted by not effectively completing the house chores. Instead, using valuable time looking at soap operas; on the phone gossiping; or must I say, roaming the streets, which is unacceptable and disrespectful in the relationship. On the other hand, when a crisis visit a relationship such as one of the individuals may have lost his/her job, which brings about a financial challenge or hardship; a change in togetherness, love and feelings—this is the time when a negative change in attitude starts to *show up* and *show out* and it shouldn't be allowed in a "genuine love" relationship. Just remember, if you should experience adversity in your relationship—that should really bring both of you closer and more loving. Not only that, in a "genuine love" relationship, the individual should feel each other's pain—in short, when one is sad and hurting, then the other one should show compassion and sympathy, as well as encourage and uplift the companion. In addition, both individuals should kneel in prayer asking the Lord for strength, assistance, favor and deliverance during those trying times. Also, during storms or adversities in a relationship, Satan and his elves (evil doers), consider that an invitation to camp out on your territory to cause confusion, attitude arousal, grudge and even hatred in your household. Yes, experiencing adversities, crisis, even tests and trials in a relationship can be stressful, painful, oppressive and depressive, but do not allow what you are experiencing interfere with your "genuine love" relationship. Both companions should together *pray harder; keep the faith; keep loving, encouraging and supporting one another.* Be confident that when the relationship remains strong and bonded, Satan and his elves have been defeated, for that's their job 24/7, to seek whom they can devour. Not only that, Satan hates a "genuine love" relationship and he will even use people (his elves) to cause confusion and division whether experiencing a crisis or not—he hates to see God involved in other people's lives or relationships and just know that Satan does exist and he never sleeps nor slumber—he's a no good and an unfriendly busybody. Satan also loves when a relationship experience adversity or a crisis because he's confident that he can make one or the other companion walk out of the relationship leaving the other individual to go through alone, physically. If this should ever happen, then the individual who departed the relationship was weak and didn't really have "genuine love" for the soul-mate. Perhaps, just in the relationship to enjoy and receive whatever the purpose, whether it was having a place to live; finance; materialistic items, romance, etc. A person that falls weak to Satan's tactics by departing the relationship during trying times doesn't have a heart nor conscious and never had genuine love—that was only a goat dressed in sheep clothing (pretense love and no good intentions in the relationship). Sometimes in a relationship while experiencing a crisis such as foreclosure; demotion; a loss of job; repossession; severe illness, or no longer able to work due to health issues—a mate departure from the relationship during this period of time not only usually causes the other mate to experience depression, but often become suicidal (wanting to kill the companion and possibly him or herself). To reiterate, a time such as this, Satan uses as an open door to cause severe damage leaving the *aggressor* having to face the legal and spiritual system. My friends, do not fall into

Satan's trap even if your mate walks out on you during your tests and trials — just know that God is there all the time and look at the situation in a *positive* manner instead of a negative one, while understanding and accepting the fact that your partner isn't your source — just a temporary provider because King Jesus is your everlasting and non-failing source and unlimited provider.

The negative view of a situation would be of Satan, also known as "Slew Foot", who will have you reflecting (also known as flashbacks) on all you have done and bought for your better-half, and Satan will instill in your mind and heart to seek revenge (hurt) by taking back everything you have bought your mate. Well, don't do that because remember, you bought it out of love which is from the heart. Keep in mind that "genuine" (true love) can't be purchased and Jesus paid that price (genuine love), for all of us when God gave him up to be crucified. Satan will also tell you to harm your mate as a token of revenge, whether it's assault, abuse, vandalism or murder. However, during a situation such as this one, always take a deep breath; pray to the Lord to remove all satanic thoughts from your mind and to give you power over Satan and your temper. You have authority over Satan so talk to him like he talks to you and tell him that he's defeated and get thee hence behind you. Also, tell him to go back to hell where he belongs because you will not be joining him. Remember, Satan uses times like these to force his elves to tell you negative information while experiencing your adversity or trials. Just tell those devilish elves when they approach you in a negative manner, that God has it all in control and you are not going to accept their opinions and suggestions because you are not a garbage dumpster, and I'm confident that they (Satan elves) will look at you as if you pricked their feelings or was being disrespectful, but you can't allow him and his workshop to breathe negative vibrations on your territory. You should always think before you react in *any* situation, about the consequences behind your reactions and just know of one consequence — if you commit a crime, you will have to do the time and pay your dimes (meaning a fine). On the other hand, in the spiritual realm, you will have to answer to God for the wrong you've done.

Now, let's look at the positive view of experiencing adversity and why it causes the other mate to depart from the relationship. Just know that regardless of what you are experiencing—God is there all the time and he doesn't put any more on his children than they can bear, so when your intimate partner departs the relationship during times of hardship or test/trial, just continue to pray for strength because that's a painful and dreadful experience. Yes, many tears will be shed, and the mate's presence will be highly missed, but look at the situation in a positive manner. For instance, maybe the Lord allowed the crisis to reveal the true nature of the individual, for the Lord knew there would be division before the crisis ever visited the relationship. Another example, perhaps the Lord probably allowed the situation to happen in order to remove the mate from the relationship because he wants to replace that person with someone who is genuine and true. A *third* illustration—sometimes the Lord allows us to go through adversities because there's a *blessing* in the *lesson* and he also wants to strengthen the relationship. Last, but not least, sometimes you can love a mate so much until all your focus and attention is on your companion and unfortunately, you don't spend any time, or enough time praying and worshipping the Lord. Unintentionally, you probably don't tithe, or partially tithe, and give in the offering like it's stated in his Holy word (the Bible); maybe because you were spending all of your funds on your mate trying to keep him/her happy, so God has to discipline your actions so that you can understand that love can't be purchased, and that your main focus should be upon him. Nevertheless, the Lord should be first in your life and not your companion. (Thou shall have no other God before me—*one of the Ten Commandments*). In summation, always put God first in your relationship and as the saying say—*a family that prays together, stays together*, is definitely true and I can attest to that. Although at some point-in-time, you may experience division in the relationship because one individual may be weaker than the other one, such as Adam and Eve, but just remember what <u>God put together</u>, there may be temporary division, but Almighty will bond the relationship back together in love and no man can destroy it.

There are people who are unhappy being alone, shacking, or in a relationship and they temporarily relieve their tension or unhappiness on another person whether it's a family member, friend or co-worker, by starting confusion and lying on another person or being loud and hostile. In a situation such as being unhappy, just remember that happiness comes from within and it takes you to be in control of your mind, thoughts and feelings. Life is what you make of it, so tell yourself just what you want in life and in a relationship and put forth the effort to accomplish it. God is not going to come down from heaven and straighten things out or put things in order for you that's why he gives us power to conquer all things. All we have to do is pray, trust in him, have the faith, patience and believe. The Lord said that if you take the first step in whatever you are trying to accomplish or perhaps, work out in a relationship whether it's family, romantic or marital, he will do the rest and when you allow God to step in, everything will be alright. With that being said, we must keep in mind that God made woman for man and we should be each other's helpmate and have understanding, love, a wonderful relationship as well as being open to what God's plan is for the relationship. You never know, he might call both of you to ministry. Always submit yourself to God just like you would do in your relationship and allow him to use both of you for his purpose and will for your lives and his glory.

Last, but not least, knowing the true meaning of love (genuine love), must I say, can have a long-lasting positive effect on a relationship if it's shared with each other cheerfully and at all times —

not just during the good times. Also, in a relationship, there must be trust in each other as well as effective communication and true love from the heart meaning when one hurts, in pain or is unhappy, then the mate should feel the pain in his/her spirit and work it out together so that both of you can be happy for genuine love is not a selfish or one way affair and in any given situation, two heads are better than one, which means when one mate is weak, then the other mate should have the weak mate's back and never allow a crack for Satan to enter in and cause confusion and violence in your relationship.

Allow me to share one of my relationship with you as a true illustration of what I'm talking about and how God is so kind, thoughtful and a great provider who will always be there for you. I met a handsome and kind young man around 2007 and had only been knowing him approximately three weeks and we weren't in a rush to be intimate, just taking our time to get to know each other. Needless to say, I had an accident at the park and broke the main bone in my left ankle and without a doubt had to have surgery and had to be off work until my ankle healed and the doctor said that a break in the main bone usually take a year to completely heal. Just know I didn't have that amount of time accrued to be off work with pay so that means my bills will be highly affected to due a financial shortage so I had started worrying and praying for the Lord to make away not knowing all the time he sent that handsome young man into my life to be a pillow for me while experiencing what I was experiencing because the Lord knew that the accident I had on the basketball court was going to happen. My mate was right there by my side at all times even when he was at work, he would call to check on me. To make a long story short, he paid my shortages; made sure grocery was stocked in the kitchen and placed the items in the appropriate places. In addition, my friend took me to my doctor's appointments and other places that I wanted to go all because he loved and cared for me and he didn't want me worrying and unhappy.

CHAPTER III

THE EIGHTEEN ATTRIBUTES OF GOD

In order to receive a better understanding of *God's genuine love*, let's keep in mind that "genuine" means pure, unselfishness, no failure, not easily angered, always trustworthy, unconditional, forgiveness and always perseveres. However, to understand the characteristics of God's genuine love, we must learn in depth about the eighteen attributes of God, which will help us to know more about the love that he shares with us, and it will also encourage us to stop the *violence* and *crime* that is taking over this world.

1) *Eternal* – God's existence is eternal because his dwelling is eternity and he knows the end from the beginning, and he's not surprised by any of our actions or behavior. Nevertheless, God promised eternal life to those who will repent of their inappropriate actions and follow him by being obedient to his word and voice.

2) *Faithfulness* – God is so truthful and faithful until he does not lie. Whatever he promises it will be presented and that's a fact which is proven in the Bible on numerous occasions. He allows every human being to be followers of Jesus because our hope for life's eternity is in God. All of the crime or violence that you played a role in will be forgiven by the promise of God, and through his faithfulness we will live with him eternally.

3) *Goodness* – God has lots of goodness that he shares with us and they are generous, compassionate and humble. Not only that, he shares his goodness with those who have engaged in a criminal act or violence, provided they repent.

4) ***Gracious*** – God is so gracious until he still blesses us even when we don't deserve it or are unworthy of his blessings. Jesus Christ is the channel for the distribution of God's grace and regardless of what you have done in life, stop the violence, repent and receive God's wonderful and awesome forgiveness.

5) ***Holiness*** – God is the one and only and his holiness distinguishes him apart from all human beings. He never has evil thoughts or intentions towards no one and he's known as Supreme Vibration. God also wants us to be holy and not allow evil thoughts to be the ruler of criminal actions or violence.

6) ***Immutability*** – Means God is the same yesterday, today and forever. His character, grace, and mercy for us will never change. Now that's genuine love when the Lord will forgive you for the wrong you have done in the past; the wrong you did today, and the wrong that you often commit because we are not perfect. So, if there's any violence or crime you've committed, ask for forgiveness, strength, and power not to commit another one.

7) ***Infinitude*** – God's power is immeasurable and infinite. No one can compare to him and he uses his infinite power in various ways in our lives. He also gives us power to overcome the snares of the devil. How awesome to have God-given power over Satan—Oh! I must say, that's "God's genuine love."

8) ***Justice*** – God's genuine love is "just", and it brings equality to everyone. When evil or a crime has been committed in this world, the criminal must receive justice. However, God is perfect and has never done any evil, and because of his genuine love, he paid the price for our evil deeds through his son Jesus who sacrificed his life on the cross for all of us.

9) *Love* – God loves us so gracefully until he did something that no other human being would ever do and that was to give his *only* begotten son, Jesus, to die for everybody so that we might have life and that more abundantly. Allow me to <u>translate</u> love to "genuine love" because no human would sacrifice their child for the people in this world. God shares his love with us each and every day when he touches us to live and see another day; has good health and strength; blesses us with the essentials of life such as: being enclosed in our right minds; having activity of our limbs, shelter, and food to nourish our bodies. With that being said, we must stop killing, shooting and injuring our sisters and brothers throughout the nation—the Lord giveth and he taketh life.

10) *Mercy* – God is merciful and his actions towards us are compassionate. However, mercy is a part of God's nature and it's endless. Although we are not perfect but are trying to live right in God's sight, he shares mercy with us when we tend to go astray or fall weak to Satan's temptation to engage in criminal activities.

(11) *Omnipotence* – Meaning God is the most powerful and he shares this genuine love with us through his power. Whatever we need whether it's healing, food, a job, or a home, he has the power to bless us with it and although God is the most powerful, he also shares some of that power with us. To illustrate, God said that we have the power to speak to our mountains (circumstances or adversaries), and they will move. In addition, God said that we have the power to defeat Satan and his tactics. However, the Lord so loves us <u>until he uses</u> his infinite power for every human being and it never needs replenishing. Not only that, let's remember that although God rested on the seventh day from all of his hard labor, doesn't mean he was weary, he was just sharing love as an example for us to rest from our labor.

(12) **Omnipresence** – God's presence is always in existence regardless of what we are going through and that's a magnificent attribute. For the scripture says that he will never leave us nor forsake us, but he will be with us until the end of the world. God is everywhere and has no boundaries, so when Slew Foot convinces you to commit a crime or indulge in violence, listen to that sweet still voice of God who is also present telling you that isn't pleasing in his sight and decline the offer from Satan. Oh! Yes, we are loved.

(13) **Omniscience** – God is perfect in all of his ways including his knowledge and therefore, there's no room for learning anything else, for he's the only one who knows all things and has knowledge that's infinite. God knows what we think or do, before we can think or perform it. Therefore, it's impossible for one to commit a crime and try to hide, so don't allow satan to enter your mind and force you to be a suspect of violence. We need to think and love as God thinks and loves.

(14) **Self-Existence** – God, today, still exists and he so loves until he waits on us to call on him through his son Jesus. God is also the Alfa and Omega — the beginning and the end.

(15) **Self-Sufficiency** - God owns everything in this world and through his genuine love he shares it with all human beings. God is perfect and has no room for improvement for he is "God" alone and doesn't need our assistance for anything. In addition, his love is so genuine until he allows every human to join together with executing his plans on this earth and to be a blessing to one another so *stop the violence.*

(16) **Sovereignty** – God is the creator and ruler of this world and he's ever most powerful. He also has the freedom to do whatever he pleases, for he's the controller of everything that happens and the reason for its existence. His genuine love still al-

lows mankind a free will to do as he/she pleases although everyone will be held accountable for their behavior and actions in life.

(17) ***Trinity*** – God revealed himself as the Father, Son and Holy Ghost, although he's one and those three cannot be separated by no means and whenever one of the three is active, in reality all three are involved. Almighty God shares that genuine love with us at all times even during our adversaries.

(18) W*isdom* – God's wisdom is so wise, and he makes no mistakes regardless of what he does. He also knows what's best for every human being such as the solution to our problems, our needs and wants. He also shares his wisdom with us by leading and guiding us to make right decisions and not be a victim of criminal acts or violence. (www.allaboutgod.com 1-18)

Briefly, let's discuss several of these attributes although all of them are very important and the *first* one is eternal: God is well-deserved to be loved and served because he's an eternal friend meaning never ending, never changing but a genuine life-time friend. To find a true friend like that in this world today, is very rare because human's flesh is weak.

Secondly is faithfulness: Jesus (through God) is really the only one to believe or have faith in because he will never deceive or lie to you but will always protect your well-being and will fulfill your prayers if what you're asking and having faith for is within his will for your life, while only having mustard seed faith. Needless to say, having faith or promise of a human will require a tremendous amount of faith because his/her word or promise can change within a twinkling of an eye.

Thirdly is mercy: Be mindful that no human being on this earth will have mercy on you when it comes to the severity of certain circumstances, but when it comes to God having mercy on you he doesn't measure it according to the severity of your circumstances, just grants you mercy.

It would be wise to familiarize yourself with these eighteen attributes and start exercising them in your mind, heart, and inner-being. Also, allow them to transform your life through your thoughts, actions, behavior, and attitude.

I would like to share a situation that I experienced, and the Lord showed me justice (*one of the eighteen attributes*) when the situation could have been injustice. During the year of 1993, I was in a domestic violence relationship and I tried everything that I possibly knew to make the relationship a peaceful one but I wasn't successful so it was time for me to depart because I refused to continue being treated worse than a wild animal, and allow my children to grow up in that kind of environment, so I packed up and move into another apartment so that I can continue to rear my children in a loving and pleasant environment. Well, my mate didn't accept that too well because I was no longer his punching bag when he wanted to take his anger and frustration out on me and I was only being a great companion and mother to my children. After begging and pleading for us (me and my children) to move back in with him and he finally accepted the fact that we weren't coming back into a hell hole, so he decided to get vicious and started harassing me; running me off the road trying to get me to stop and talk to him; leaving threatening letters on my door saying what he's going to do if we (me and my children) didn't come back to so-call home. Well, one night Satan's elf decided to carry out the satanic assignment that Satan planted in my x-companion's mind and when it happened, all evidence were visible along with eye-witnesses and the legal actions that I had taken against him, which made a "could have been" injustice situation a justice situation and God was my judge and he delivered me from all injustice consequences. Yes, all of his attributes are amazing.

CHAPTER IV

WHAT CAUSES VIOLENT BEHAVIOR IN HUMANS

You would normally think of violence taken place only in communities, streets, and wars against other countries, but violence has rapidly expanded into other parts of the world such as small towns, schools, churches, businesses, and rural areas in which millions of victims have been affected due to a serious injury (injuries) or murdered (gunned down). With that being said, *Three tragic accidents that included violence and criminal actions will be discussed and these accidents are also used as comparison or contrasting scenarios pointing out the possible causes and motives of such ungodly actions, along with illustrating how to have control of your actions and mind by thinking about God's genuine love and how he wants all human beings to share it with each other.*

First, we will explore the "The Boston Bombing". This tragic, ungodly, and unlawful accident took place during the Boston Marathon in Boston, Massachusetts on April 15, 2013, by two brothers originally from Russia—the oldest was 26-years of age, who was an unpleasant role model for his younger brother who was 19-years-old (the criminal survivor of the accident). According to the New Haven Article, the two brothers were immigrants from a well-known area of violence and their family roots stretch to Russian Republic of Chechnya, which has been a wellspring of terrorism over the years. Nevertheless, an author suspects that the condemnation of Harry Potter's books and movies by Sheik Mohammed could have motivated the 26-year-old criminal to plan the Boston Bombing. However, it's highly suspected that the Marathon Bombing by the two criminal brothers was domestic instead of terrorism. Although the brothers were reared in a surrounding of violence, which was a part of their culture, apparently, they were never taught differently, or the meaning of love. The brothers also didn't have any compassion, a humble heart or conscious, if so, they would've thought twice about injuring and killing innocent people. Just know, some people doesn't care or have any remorse when they harm or kill another individual.

Please be reminded that regardless of the negative and detrimental culture or environment you are reared in or around, as you mature, start researching on how to change your lifestyle into a positive, clean one and how to have control over all negative thoughts. Also, start socializing with positive people and around descent environments. In addition, as you mature, start learning about God's genuine love and the Ten Commandments. Always remember and exercise "Do unto others as you will have them to do unto you." Also, keep in mind that the Creator gave us life and only he has the authority to end life.

According to the Christian Science Article, Terrorism Experts stated that the bombing could have been targeted at Al Qaeda and other factors that the attack was carried out on April 15th was due to the federal income tax deadline and what in Massachusetts is Patriot Day — could also suggest the work of a disgruntled lone wolf or domestic anti-government groups. Also, a national security stated on CNN that the attack could be the work of right-wing extremists. In addition, for the so-called patriot groups, anything from Tax Day to the hated national debate on gun regulations could have been triggers for such an attack. Another possible motive for the Marathon bombing, according to the Christian Science Monitor Article, there could have been two influences that triggered the two brothers to carry out the bombing in Boston near the finish line and they were: (1) their connection with their heritage in violence-torn Chechnya, with its brand of jihadist militancy. (2) Their possible feelings of displacement as immigrants in the U.S. Another facet of the story appears to be the question of how long the younger brother had been following his older brother as a role model.

An uncle of the brothers once said he grew concerned about the older sibling after a 2009 phone conversation during which the younger brother said he had chosen "God's business" over work or school. The older sibling said he then contacted a family friend who told him the younger gunman had been influenced by a recent convert to Islam, according to the Associated Press. Needless to say, the brothers had been in the U.S. for about a decade, but retained an interest in their homeland, Chechnya.

In my opinion, it seems as if the troubled younger adult experienced some form of psychological problem in his childhood. Maybe the brothers didn't receive the attention and care needed by one or both of their parents for whatever reason. Or, perhaps, the older brother probably received more attention from their parent(s) than the younger troublesome son, leaving him to feel unloved, uncared for and unwanted. So, as the younger brother matures, his *behavior* and all other pessimistic thoughts had begun to escalate and that could be one possibility why the father and the older brother separated from him and their mother. Nevertheless, for the younger gunman to target children at school as a prey, possibly he could have had some bad experiences during his school days such as being bullied, false accused, or maybe he stayed in trouble. On the other hand, he probably was jealous of the other students because of their lifestyle; their style of dressing, and/or maybe some of his friends may have been the teacher's favorite and received plenty of attention.

I boldly say with emphasis, that parents are not the only influence on a child's behavior, although parents rear the child in the appropriate manner by teaching him/her about the facts of life; how to be mannerable, and other values of life. However, there are still other factors that can have a negative effect on a child's behavior causing the young one to think violent, become violent, and indulge in criminal activities. To begin, the first factor is media violence that's shown on television, or at the movie theater. A maturing child shouldn't be exposed to violent media because he/she learns from it and feels that kind of behavior is acceptable in this society. However, a child does not know how to differentiate *pretense* television violence from real life. With that being said, to help prevent a child from having a violent behavior, let me share with you two characteristics that predict the development of aggression assessed by physical violence and externalizing behaviors. Secondly, let's become knowledgeable about the risk factors for violence in this world:

I. **Characteristics**

A. **Physical Discipline (by parents and caretakers)**

There's a proper way and an improper way to discipline a child, and the proper way is highly recommended because the kind of aggression used to punish a child will incubate in their memories and if the punishment is highly aggressive such as using profanity, calling them unpleasant names, and child abuse, then that's the pattern the child will follow throughout his/her life causing violent and abusive behavior towards others.

B. **A Child's Inhibited Temper**

According to Science Reports (Vol. 300, 20 June 2003), Researchers (5), stated that children with an inhibited temperament tend to be timid with people, objects, and situations that are novel or unfamiliar, whereas uninhibited children spontaneously approach novel persons, objects, and situations. These behavioral differences in young children were accompanied by distinctive physiological differences, including differences in heart rate and heart rate variability, papillary dilation during cognitive tasks, vocal cord tension when speaking under moderate stress, and salivary cortisol levels.

In addition, Dr. Iris Borowsky stated the following risk factors in our society that can cause children to become cruel or violent:

II. Risk Factors

A. Having Access to Guns

1) economic deprivation
2) neighborhood violence
3) social prejudice

B. In Families
1) violent environment
2) substance abuse
3) lack of communication, caring, and bonding

C. In Schools
1) lack of achievement
2) lack of connectedness
3) peer pressure
4) sense of failure

According to Dr. Kathy Seifert's experience and research, she identified numerous factors that determined human behavior and whether a person is at risk for developing violent tendencies. These factors include biological traits, family bonding, individual characteristics, intelligence and education; child development, peer relationships, cultural shaping, and resiliency. Dr. Kathy Seifert also stated that each factor of a person's life or makeup can affect and be affected by another factor. When the accumulation of negative factors (such as maltreatment, chaotic neighborhoods, or psychological problems) and the absence of positive factors, (such as opportunities to be successful, adults who provide encouragement, or a resilient temperament) reach a threshold, that's when violence is more likely to erupt as a means of coping with life's problems. We must understand and realize that factors, whether they're negative or positive, play a very important and critical role in the lives of children, youths and young adults, so the parents are accountable for the kind of model their child(ren) will be and parents should never allow negative factors to overpower the positive ones in their family relationship with their child (ren).

Through additional researching, you can seek more knowledge on the information previous listed that will assist you with recognizing a violent and criminal behavior in children or helping children to avoid the risk factors that lead to violence. However, we must realize that it's the parent's responsibility to fulfill this important role in protecting their kids from all types of violent involvement. Another factor of importance is having a close parent-family relationship by showing care and connection because children should feel that their parents love them; are close to them, and they should be able to have fun with their parents with all due respect *(Dr. Iris Borowsky)*. In addition to teaching your child the core values of life, she/he should be taught about God's genuine love, which will, without a doubt, stray them away from violence and criminal activities. However, teaching a child about the Ten Commandments principles is a great foundation that should be instilled in a child as he/she is maturing instead of waiting until he/she is older.

Secondly, is the Sandy Hook Elementary Massacre that took place in Newton, Connecticut in 2012. In this accident, according to *Time.com Article*, the young gunman had a troubled relationship with his mother. However, this shooting was described as one of the worst shootings in American history. Also, according to *Time.com*, the 20-year-old first killed his mother; 20 children and 6 adults before killing himself at the Sandy Hook Elementary School in Newton, Connecticut. It was concluded that the gunman acted alone and according to the evidence, it's believed that no other person conspired with the shooter to commit these crimes or aided and abetted him in doing so.

The gunman's mother said in November 2012, that she and her younger son (the criminal), only communicated by email despite living in the same house and he was not allowed in his room. In fact, some witnesses told investigators that the young troublesome gunman did not have an emotional connection to his mother. Needless to say, according to *Time.com*, the mother extensively cared for her son and told people that she decided not to work so she would have more time to take care of him. Sadly to say, the estranged father and older brother had no contact with the young gunman since 2010 and 2012 according to (http://web.ebscohost).

According to *Time.com*, the young man was also interested in other school shootings. There's a possibility that the shooter had a mental health condition and refused to take treatment for it. In addition, according to *USA Today*, the 20-year-old psychiatric gunman was deeply troubled and had a violent soaked culture. It was also stated that people with guns kill people and that most disturbed people should be separated from the deadliest weapons. In addition, in *USA Today* assistance with the gun lobby is geared towards presidential leadership and Congress. Nevertheless, most gunmen have delusional, threatening or violent behavior.

Thirdly – Florida Neighborhood Watchman (Caucasian/Hispanic) vs 17-year-old African American teenager. A Florida neighborhood watchman in Sanford, Florida had a confrontation with a Florida teenager who was an African American, which led to the teen's death. On February 26, 2012, according to the *International Business Times Article*, the 911 calls that the watchman made characterized his zealous, angry mind-set, and "ill will." It was also stated that the calls showed the context in which the Caucasian/Hispanic watchman sought out his encounter with the African American 17-year-old, (although he was legally told not to do so), that was heard on the 911 recording moments before he shot the teen, a profanity-laced string of words. An additional statement by the prosecutor stated the gunman shot the teen for the worst of all, no apparent reason only because he wanted to, according to the *International Business Times Article*.

It also appears that the watchman has a psychological ailment such as temperament, anger, a lack of self-control, and a high level of ego, in which he likes to play the role of macho man who needs no leading or instructions regarding a situation—just handle it on his own without legal authority instructions. Needless to say, a person such as the watchman, not only need mental or psychiatric assistance—he needs to be introduced to God's genuine love and the Ten Commandments. It's imperative that he must also learn to love every race, gender and sex. Above all, the triggerman must also ask God, the father, for forgiveness for disobeying the Ten Commandments and he must also learn to follow legal orders to <u>prevent crime</u> in this world. However, people should realize when a life is taken from this earth due to crime, that's not pleasing in the eyesight of God. With that being said, this brutal crime could have been avoided if the watchman would have followed the orders of the 911 dispatcher and those orders were to stop following the teen, and don't get out of his vehicle, according to several medias.

Since the murder verdict was in favor of the neighborhood gunman, he must watch his back due to the threats of his life being taken, according to media and articles. Not only that, his character is well-known by others in the world due to medias and people from across the world uniting to march for justice against a crime that could have been prevented. According to a news article, the watchman may not ever be employed again due to his criminal actions. I must say, although it may be tough for him in the workforce, there's hope for any situation and God Almighty is the answer to the gunman's hopelessness. He must *first* repent of his sins (which is the crime committed and his disobedience of the Ten Commandments), then open his heart and mind to accept a dramatic change in his life (such as his character, personality, attitude, etc.). *Next*, he must willfully submit his life to Christ and ask the Lord to show him his godly ways and the purpose for his life. *Finally,* the murderer must learn and instill in his heart the meaning of love and "God's genuine love", then begin implementing it in his life daily towards <u>all</u> human beings.

Let's gain some insight on violence and crime even though they seem to be related or connected. The definition of <u>violence</u>: A behavior involving physical force intended to hurt, damage, or kill someone or something. Next, the definition of <u>crime</u>: An action or activity that's considered to be evil, shameful or wrong. Let's be reminded that it's God's genuine love that will have a <u>positive effect</u> on violence and crime, which have a large portion of the market share in this world. According to FBI reporting, property crimes were an estimated *8,632,512* in 2014. However, the 2013 statistics show the estimated rate of violent crime was *367.9* offenses per 100,000 inhabitants, and the property crime rate was *2,730.7* offenses per 100,000 inhabitants. (www.fbi.gov/news/stories)

Additionally, in 2012, the rate for homicide was 4.7 percent per 100,000. Also, in 2012, according to the Bureau of Justice Statistics (BJS) and the National Crime Victimization Survey (NCVS), violent and property crime rates increased for U.S. residents age 12 or older. Not only that, but the overall violent crime rate (which includes rape or sexual assault, robbery, aggravated and simple assault) rose from *22.6* victimizations per 1,000 persons in 2011 to *26.1* in 2012. However, some crimes are not reported because victims see the event as a personal matter (a fight between friends or family members); a theft that the victim considers minor, or the victims' belief that law enforcements cannot resolve the issue (a theft where the likelihood of getting property back or resulting in the arrest of the offender is unlikely). As we can see, according to statistics, <u>crime is rising</u> more than decreasing so that's why every one globally, must come together and pray; love one another; care for one another, and generously help one another directly and indirectly because millions of crimes are being committed throughout the world. (www.fbi.gov/news/stories /latest crime)

Surely, by exercising God's genuine love, which is the **"root solution"** for violence and crime — can have a <u>positive effect</u> on the crime rate in this world. Nonetheless, starting today, recite this prayer and make this confession with me: *Lord, in the name of Jesus, help me to love myself and others. Give me strength to avoid the snares of the devil and whisper to me what you will have me to speak to others who are confused and contemplating a crime. In the name of Jesus, I pray, Amen.* Confession: *I'm partnering with Author Ruby to help cease the violence and starting today, I will always mention one or more attributes of God and see what I can do to help someone to avoid violence and crime. I'm an advocate for "Stopping the violence" in this world.*

Yes, I have crazy faith and strong belief that with God all things are possible and the crime rate can decrease to 0% in this world and to make this a reality, <u>everybody</u> must come together on one accord to pray, incorporate God's genuine love in your lives, and put forth the effort to cease violence and crime, along with welcoming "change". We must also realize that sometimes we can be our own enemy, so don't allow Satan to breathe on that and transform evil thoughts into criminal action. Satan is the father of crimes and he's not your friend because a true and loving friend will not instill violent thoughts in a person's mind. Tell Satan to go back to the pit of hell where he belongs because committing a crime will not incarcerate your blessed and valuable time. On a daily basis, rebuke Satan's violent and criminal actions by reciting this phrase out loud or within yourself: *God is my source, strength, and friend — I refuse to forsake him for an unloving, uncaring, goat dressed in sheep's clothing.*

There are numerous types of crimes such as robbery, theft, murder, carjacking, burglary, bullying, kidnapping, abuse, assault, and domestic violence that are overpowering this world. Did you know that all crimes are unethical, unacceptable, illegal, and are subject to criminal and spiritual disciplinary action? Some people commit crimes on purpose for *money, love, and jealousy*. However, there are several well-known factors of crime, such as alcohol and illegal drugs. Perhaps, most people who were arrested for crimes they committed were either highly intoxicated or drug overdosed. Another key factor for crime is the *environment* that an individual is reared. If the individual is seeking to survive and sees his/her role model committing a crime, then that individual may feel that's the right road to survival.

Normally drug addicts commit crimes against property such as theft (house or car burglary) and robbery, whether it's a business or an innocent person. The reason being for this crime is the drug addicts have probably run out of money to support their habits (a "must have") therefore, instant funds are needed so the criminal steals something of value from a victim in exchange for money, whether it's a sell on the streets or to a pawn shop. However, people also commit crimes because of poverty and other unethical habits they must support. Another reason for committing crimes is due to greed and jealousy, or to impress others, and because they are too lazy to enter the workforce.

Have you often wondered why do people commit crimes or engage in violence and crimes? Well, violent crimes can be attributed to biological causes like hormones and certain blood abnormalities, even sociological causes like unemployment, poverty, and psychological problems are also contributing factors. Another violent crime which is in the high percentage bracket is *domestic violence* and it's usually committed due to intimacy and the partner loses control of his/her emotions. Not only men, but women are known to be abusers, but not like that of man who's known to be the one to physically abuse the woman and perhaps even kill her.

Now, when we speak of *murder*, the crime is usually or normally committed by someone that's well-known or affiliated with the victim and the crime is highly committed due to drugs or alcohol, money, love, envious, or a similar motive or factor. Not only that, some killings are also gang ring or drug related. Lastly, there are serial killers who don't have a motive—they just choose people randomly to kill and the condition of this type of behavior is affected by biological and environmental factors, which is well-known as a mental illness and some early warning signs of a person who could be experiencing the behavior of a serial killer are being cruel to animals, bed wetting, and arson.

Another reason why people commit crimes is actually due to psychological reasons and a possibility of having *no knowledge about the law*. Nevertheless, crimes happen when an opportunity presents itself, and people can avoid being a victim of crime by becoming aware of their surroundings; being cautious; and remain focused. Some precautions to prevent being victimized are: Lock all doors in your vehicle and home; don't leave any valuable items visible in your car or home; and never wander the streets or alley at night alone. *Anger* is another killer if it's not controlled, and most homicides or killings are done by people being under the influence of drugs and/or alcohol. However, people who are under the influence are incoherent, very strong and very angry. Nevertheless, anger is a factor that can cause some form of violence if it's transformed into action. People who have cognitive control of their mind and well-being have a great chance of avoiding violence. To have control over your life and keep it functioning exceptionally well, you must <u>always</u> have self-control because your brain opens opportunities for an assortment of influences to migrate.

This knowledge will help you to recognize people with a violent or criminal demeanor and how to help them or avoid them. In addition, this knowledge will also, hopefully, prevent humans from becoming violent, or if already violent—how to change that demeanor and how to control, or not indulge in criminal activities. Although most violence and crime are being committed by youths and younger adults in this world, you may often ask these particular questions:

a) *What is wrong with the people in this world today?*
b) *What's causing people to commit crimes or become violent?*
c) *What was the motive for that crime or violent act?*
d) *Who's going to step up and do something to decrease or stop the violence and criminal activities in this world?*
e) *Who's responsible for controlling crime and violence in this world?*
f) *Exactly what can be implemented to stop crime and violence in this world?*

I must say that law enforcements can't always keep all of our communities safe because there aren't enough of them to be every where. If you are like me, my heart and passion for violence and crime to cease is not just for my city, state, or community, but for the world, which includes all races, states, counties, countries, etc. As you can see, committing crimes and participating in violence seem to be a norm for some people often reacting on their impulses, or out of anger by harming other human beings who are major predators. Not animals, plants, or building being the major criminal predator, but again, I say it's human beings, which is very drastic, sorrowful and devastating.

Whether you know it or not, all violence has different characteristics or factors, which makes them indifferent. In fact, some abnormal people who become violent may have an impulsive behavior; suffer a drug or alcohol disinhibition, or perhaps violent human beings may be dealing with a serious mental illness. Other reasons why humans may become violent are due to some form of hatred against another human being, or perhaps, some kind of unpleasant experience, or possible revenge. Additionally, people may become violent due to an unordinary strange home environment; family factors including a lack of attention; alcohol and drugs, anger reliever; or possibly peer pressure. Without a doubt, uncontrollable actions can also cause violent actions. Last, but not least, people are also known to act on violent thoughts that roams and dingles through their minds such as actors/actresses who are violent on television shows and in movies; planned violence; or violent video games, which includes fighting, shooting, drinking and smoking, just to name several. I highly suggest that people disengage or don't watch violent activities due to a lack of cognitive control—can't distinguish reality from fake action, and they often rely and depend on television, media, movies, etc. as a role model for their lives. Even listening to violent rhetoric or music makes people more inclined to act out of their character or become violent due to a lack of self-control and a lack of knowledge for reality.

Allow me to share my view of rearing a child. Whether you know it or not, rearing a child plays a very important role in the life of that child. However, I can truly say that the rearing I received from my precious grandmother, along with my loving and caring stepfather, was the greatest and their teaching and discipline are the patterns I chose to rear my two children. My two role models (grandma and stepfather), taught me everything in life there was to know as I was growing up such as, being obedient and respectful to everyone; the facts of life and what to expect in life; the challenges that will come upon me in life and how to prepare for them—just to name several. Not only that, I wasn't allowed to socialize with children that had no respect; that were troublesome and could be a bad influence in my life. I will not go into full details about the greatest rearing I could have ever received, and even today, I still follow the principles and rearing I received from grandma and step-dad. In addition, as I grew older, I always called my grandmother's and stepfather's teaching, leading and guidance—sermons. Wow! What love, care, and concern those angels had for lonely me. Unexpectedly, the Lord called my grandmother home when I was about sixteen, and he called my stepfather home when I was about twenty-years-old. Without a doubt, those two deaths were very hard to cope with because those angels were so deeply rooted in my heart and as of today, I still have thoughts, love, feelings and compassion for them, and it's the Almighty God who has helped me to make it thus far and he's continuously keeping my feeble mind and heart strengthened as I travel this journey because he does nothing to hurt us and his ways are not our ways. One thing we must realize and be thankful for, is when God blesses us with love ones, friends, companion and children. For God's sake, never get too attached to them although that's impossible not to do, because God is only sharing them with us for a short period of time, then they must ascend to their eternal home.

Although the Lord called those two angels home (grandma and step-dad) during my teenage and young adult life, he allowed them plenty of time to mold me into a strong, compassionate black woman who is intelligent, respectful, mannerable, loving, and has been well-taught about the all-powerful Father and how to trust in him. The Lord said in his word that he will never leave us nor forsake us, and I can without a doubt, attest to that while on this life's journey. After the Lord called my two guardian angels home who will always be in my heart, he blessed me with another loving angel. Isn't God good! Oh Yes, she took me under her wings and was a very loving and caring mother to me. She continued and reiterated the sermon that my grandmother and stepfather preached to me, in which right today I still call her, respect her, and love her as my mother. She made sure that I was taken care of, and not only that, she made sure I was employed. That's another special person (Moma), that I adore and truly love. That adorable woman will always remain in my heart and prayers, as well as on my mind.

Nevertheless, parents only know how to rear their children according to the way they were reared, whether it was abusive; in an unpleasant environment such as drugs and profanity being uttered. In return, as a child matures to an adult and birth a baby, then that young adult rears the child according to his/her parent(s) role model. Above all, rearing most definitely does start from the home, and it will be displayed by the child in public such as school, at the shopping mall, restaurants, etc. Parents should teach their child(ren) how to love themselves and others. However, although parents tries very hard to keep their child(ren) from around negative influences such as criminal and violent activities shown on television; disrespectful children; a hostile environment; violent movies; unpleasant rap music; etc., as the child gradually reach the adulthood stage in life he/she might decides to take a step into that destructive and unpleasant life only to see what he/she has been abandoned from. Also, *peer pressure* can pull a well-mannered individual into the so called, "haunted house", or, "nightmare on Elm St." Nevertheless, it's the child's decision, and all the parent can do is pray for him/her. Without a doubt, I can boldly say that if you instill *good values* into your child and teach him/her the true facts about life such as, being well-mannered; respect; etc., regardless of the life your child chooses to live or temporary explore, the true values in that individual will never fade away and at some point-in-time, the child will return to the lifestyle and rearing that he/she is accustomed to.

Needless to say, my message to all of God's precious human beings, whether you were reared in a pleasant or unpleasant environment or your childhood's life was pleasant or unpleasant — take the initiative to learn about "God's genuine love" and exercise it in your daily living as well as share it with others. Regardless of your age, don't allow peer pressure, satanic voices and thoughts have control over your decision-making. Yes, everybody has made bad decisions in life and perhaps, rode on the wrong train track, but it's not too late to catch that *positive* and *Godly* train that will lead you to a land of success and peace. *In contrast*, the negative train will lead you into violence, crime, and incarceration.

Remember to always stay in control of your mind and thoughts; always think before you react in any given situation; always ask God for power and strength to overcome the snares of the devil and rebuke all negative thoughts that come to your mind pressuring you to make them become reality—that's the work and spirit of Satan the manipulator. For example, if you are denied a job position, whether it's your first job or an application for a promotion—do not allow denial to negatively affect your self-esteem or to escalate hatred and anger toward the person in charge such as a supervisor or manager. Be mindful at all times that the escalation of hatred and anger in your mind and heart leaves room for violent thoughts toward the person in charge. That's when Satan comes in and tells you that taking violent action will get what you want, which isn't the right resolution for denial. On the other hand, the *root solution* for denial is to be in control of your temper and calmly accept denial as a delay in a job or promotion because God knows more than we do, and that job or promotion just might not be the best fit for you, so just say, "Thank you Jesus", and keep moving forward. Another illustration, jealousy and envy are two tools that Satan strongly uses to manipulate a person into becoming violent and to commit a crime. For instance, there are people in the world who works hard to have nice materialistic items such as a car, clothes and even a home, and you have those who don't want to work to support themselves, so they feel that unlawfully stealing, robbing, damaging other people's belongings is the right thing to do in life because of envious and jealousy. Be informed that in the eyesight of God and the law, envious and jealousy really can cause unpleasant consequences when they are used toward a person unethically and unlawfully, so don't yield to the voice of Satan or his elves. In addition, just know Satan never sleeps nor slumbers and he does have a workshop of elves waiting to carry out his demonic commands and satanic orders. Don't give in to his offer or become his flunky because he has nothing good to reward you for the crime he persuades you to illegally commit. "Think" before you do and yield not to deceitful temptation. God loves you and his soft still voice is the righteous one to obey and just know that God made the universe, therefore, he owns every single thing in it and he's always waiting and willing to give you your heart's desire, all you have to do is pray, seek him and be patient for he has supernatural ways of providing for you and all you have to do is have faith only the size of a mustard seed and trust him because becoming violent and committing a crime such as assault or murder will escalate the situation instead of resolving it. Be mindful that committing a crime will cost you your valuable time and all your dimes in addition to other unpleasant consequences that you will have to pay which are not favorable ones.

I would like to share with you a scenario that I experienced in the workplace and how the Lord showed up and showed out on my behalf and right today, I still thinks about how he made my enemy my footstool and gave me victory over a spiritual warfare. Don't let Satan persuade you into believing that his little muscles are stronger than God's strength because they are not. He's nothing but a weak serpent who lost my battle against God. To begin, a new CEO was appointed to the council and she tried to terminate all of the soldiers (employees who had been there for years). She was really on a rampage and harassing us soldiers, so I put a sign on my wall saying, "Greater is he that is within me is greater than he that is in the world". I also had a sign up that said, "No weapon formed against me with prosper." She saw those signs in my area and asked me to take them down and leave. In short, after all of her satanic work towards us soldiers, the Lord got rid of her and I was compensated for the days she suspended me for. Look at mighty King Jesus, the one who will never lose a battle and he enjoys making Satan bow down and tuck his tail and run, hey, hey, King Jesus will fight and win any battles that you may have whether they are work-related, family-related or relationship related—just know no battle is too hard for God to conquer and he also said that we are conquers through him only believe.

WHAT CAUSES CHILDREN TO BE AGGRESSIVE AND VIOLENT

There are numerous factors that determine children's behavior and they are: The traits from biological parents; the characteristics of the child; how well is the family bonding; how well is the child's development; does the child have peer relationship; the child's education along with his/her intelligence; and last but not least, the child's culture. In addition, these factors can also determine if a child is at risk for a development of violent tendencies, although every child is different and the factors previous listed can be affected by another factor. However, when negative factors grow from one to many and overpowering the positive factors (such as parental encouragement and love, a mild and controllable temper, successful opportunities, etc.), that can cause violence as a mean of coping with the problem(s) in life.

Realizing the importance of negative and *positive* factors and how they seriously affect the lives of children, youths, and young adults, can make a great difference in a child's life by enforcing the positive factors and eliminating the negative factors. Another possible lead for children becoming aggressive and violent is they may have grown up in or around violence such as: in their homes, city, community or neighborhood. Not only that, some analysts assume that demographic and socioeconomic factors account for most child aggression. Other factors that can predict aggression are: (1) harsh physical punishment in the family (2) inhibition (3) peer victimization predicted amount of aggression and, (4) low self-esteem predicted amount of aggression, but not as strongly as the other factors.

Some of the reasons why humble children become extremely violent and/or cruel are due to: (1) being exposed to media violence and children learn from what they observe on TV, in life, or their surroundings and environment. Needless to say, children really can't distinguish real violence from television pretense violence, so it would be healthy if you don't allow them to watch violence. With that being said, parents are not the only influence regarding a child's behavior but play a major role. (2) Some children don't know or think about the consequences for their actions, or perhaps, haven't been taught or lectured about the consequences. (3) children who show a violent behavior need help immediately. However, some violence is due to impulsive behavior; the disinhibition by drugs or alcohol; mental illness; hate; or revenge. Although we may not ever know "exactly why" to any act of violence, we can continue to try and <u>prevent the violent and criminal behavior.</u>

Have you ever realized that a child doesn't have to be a specific age to indulge in violence? Did you know that a pre-school individual can be a participant in violence? Without a doubt or any hesitation, a sign of violence in a child at any age needs to be taken seriously. Not only that, a child who displays explosive or unruly behavior is the most troublesome for parents and teachers to oversee. Nevertheless, there are numerous reasons linked to childhood aggression such as: Were parents together during childbirth; poverty level income, and lastly, whether the mother's side of the family has a genetic pattern of physical abuse and antisocial behavior. Nonetheless, when a child seems to be at risk, immediate assistance is needed, which could lead to violence prevention. On the other hand, there are two known factors regarding how to prevent a violent behavior and they are: The environment that a person surrounds him/herself and genetics. Although violence and disruptive behavior might be genetic, that's no excuse for an individual (child or an adult) to follow that pattern. A person must be taught how to love him/herself and in return, the individual will share love and compassion. I can attest that genetics doesn't always play a major role in a child's or person's behavior or action. For example, my mother was an alcoholic and even drank while carrying my siblings and me, but all praise be to God, I never had a desire to drink nor smoke even though I was surrounded in that kind of unhealthy environment during my childhood and young adult life. Not only that, my paternal and stepfather were also heavy drinkers and again, that had no effect on me and that's factual, so some excuses that some people use just to continue to drink or smoke claiming it's hereditary and genetic and that's why they can't stop the bad habits, is a very poor excuse. As time progressed and I was going through my maturity stages, people would often ask me if I drink or smoke because some of them did both—I would always tell them no because I never had a desire to. I also told them how people looked and acted when they smoked for instance, when I saw smokers, they looked like a dragon blowing out smoke through their nostril and mouth, which made them looked so ugly. Now the drinkers or alcoholics, wow! They really looked spooky and like awful smelling zombies. I also paid attention to the difference in a person when he/she drinks and when the individual is sober. Oh! My! What a great difference in the appearance, speech and behavior when one is intoxicated or perhaps on cloud nine from inputting drugs in their bodies. I'm a living witness and I can truly say that you can do and accomplish anything you want in life by having faith in God and utilizing the power that he gave you to have control over whatever your mind wants, whether it's alcohol or drugs. People, it's imperative that you learn to control your mind and what it tells you to do because it's only Satan behind the scene brainwashing you by making you believe it's very hard to stop all bad habits. He'll also tell you there's no hope for ending your bad habits, which is a satanic lie because with God all things are possible, so choose today to start having control and not let Satan control your heart and mind for he doesn't mean you any good and will never tell you to do good or treat one another good. God gave you power over Satan so make it up in your mind that you'll stop your bad habits and discontinue your relationship with those who are doing what you are trying to stop doing due to peer pressure and them not respecting your efforts.

SEVEN CRIMES THAT CAUSES VIOLENT ACTIONS

I: Assault

Aggravated assault is a serious criminal offense and we hear of it on a regular basis whether it's on the news, someone talking about it, or actually witnessing a person assaulting another person. Even though we hear of this word quite often, let's gain a better understanding of it through its definition. As stated, a person is guilty of aggravated assault if he/she attempts to cause serious injury to another or causes such injury purposely, knowingly, or recklessly under circumstances manifesting extreme indifference to the value of human life; or attempt to cause or purposely or knowingly cause body injury to another with a deadly weapon. In all jurisdiction statutes punish such aggravated assault as assault with intent to murder (rob, kill, or rape) and assault with a dangerous or deadly weapon, according to the Farlex Free Dictionary.

II. Bribery

First, several definitions of bribery and they are: (1) When a person wants something, or something to happen and he/she pays someone to help make it happen; (2) When someone wants to keep a secret and bribes someone, they usually end up paying regularly to satisfy the beholder of the secret; (3) Bribery, a form of corruption is an act implying money or gift given that alters the behavior of the recipient. Not only that, bribery constitutes a crime and is defined by Black's Law Dictionary as the offering, giving, receiving, or soliciting of any item of value to influence the actions of an official or other person in charge of a public or legal duty. The bribe is the gift bestowed to influence the recipient's conduct. However, it may be in the form of money, goods, rights, an action, property, preferment, privilege, object of value, advantage, or merely a promise or undertaking to induce or influence the action, vote, or influence of a person in an official or public capacity and (4) The making of illegal payment or bribes to persons in official positions as a mean of influencing their decisions. Bribery of a public official is a *felony*.

Bribery is mainly taken place among government officials, other countries and international businesses. To bribe also means payment, or other favors to induce others to act in favor of the bribe givers. Most bribes are given to public officials to make them change the rules or break the laws that were made for the common good. As they undermine the common good for personal benefit, they're unworthy of the public's trust and become accomplices of Satan and his elves. In addition, there are two types of bribes that are well-known according to Shahabuddin, and they are: *Whitemail*, which is used to induce an official to perform an illegal or uneconomic act. This type of bribe is given to politicians or major government officials and is common in many developed countries. The second type of bribery is called *lubrication*, which is used to expedite or facilitate a normal governmental approval of a legal transaction. Lubrication bribe is a routine in many developing countries and solicited mainly by minor government officials. However, in some countries, officials resort to extortion which is an act by an official to seek payment from an individual or corporation to perform a lawful act. (Shahabu-2002)

Whether a society considers bribery to be morally wrong depends on its culture. Perhaps, it's a norm to brainwash children as they grow up to work for the government, so they can accumulate wealth through graft or favors. Other cultures disapprove accepting bribes or favors and label them as unethical. Thus, culture determines if a country will condone bribes and that's why it's difficult to say if that kind of behavior is ethical globally. I must inform you that regardless of what countries approve bribery to be ethical, the Bible states that bribery is unethical. In *Exodus 23:8*, it states, "And you shall take no bribe, for a bribe blinds the clear-sighted and subverts the cause of those who are in the right." The book of _Proverbs 15:27_ states, "Whoever is greedy for unjust gain troubles in his own household, but he who hates bribes will live." _Ecclesiastes 7:7_ states, "Surely oppression makes a wise man mad and a gift destroyeth the heart." Additional scriptures you can read regarding the corruption of bribery are:

>   (**1**) I-Timothy 6:10; (**2**) Proverbs 17:23; (**3**) Amos 5:12;
>   (**4**) Psalms 26:10; (**5**) Isaiah 5:23; (**6**) Proverbs 10:2; and
>   (**7**) Deuteronomy 16:19.

III. Bullying

First, I would like to share my perspective of bullying, then I will share additional beneficial information with you regarding this topic. This unethical behavior not only affects children but adults as well and there are numerous types of bullying such as cyber, physical, verbal, and social media. My definition of bullying is when a person (whether a kid or an adult), tries to intimidate another individual by threats, aggressiveness, mean, bossy, and/or violence. Bullies can be a group of individuals or just one, and they are known to attack those who look or seem to be intelligent, humble, kind-hearted, well-off, or those who seem incompetent or weak-minded.

Bullies are known to accomplish their mission towards other chosen individuals by being in control or just prove a point to gain public recognition by fighting, threats, or other types of violence. Not only that, but a person or group of people who seeks preys to bully are usually filled with jealousy, envious and the environment in which a bully was reared could be a possible motive for the improper behavior. There have been instances where a victim of bullying was beaten severely or to death. However, I suggest that if someone tries to bully you meaning try to instill fear within you just to accomplish a planned mission — stand boldly and look the bully in the eyes and ask these questions only to get the disturbed individual to recognize and be aware that a bullying behavior is unethical and not of God. Here are the four questions to be asked: (1) Do you realize that bullying is the works of demonic spirits using you to accomplish Satan's task? (2) Will you take the time to realize that Satan is abusing your reputation and labeling you as an elf in his workshop? (3) Do you realize that you are a human-being and not a wild beast and bullying isn't showing care and love for yourself nor the victim? (4) Lastly, do you realize that bullying carries consequences with the legal system and God? Will you please stop the satanic behavior towards your fellow sisters and brothers and "think" before you "act"? (Meaning allowing the satanic behavior to lead you into violence and committing a crime).

Needless to say, bullying can cause severe trauma to the victim physically, emotionally and psychologically. However, parents should educate their child(ren) at an early age about bullying, which is an unethical and violent behavior, so that the child(ren) will not become a victim of bullying nor become a bully. Also, parents with school age children should take the time to listen to their child(ren) when they talk about what's going on in their environment such as school and stay abreast of what the child(ren) is saying. Never wait until a situation has escalated, then try to resolve the problem—always address small issues before they become serious problems or accidents. In addition, at all times, make your child(ren) feel comfortable expressing their thoughts and feelings as well as what's happening in their surroundings. The Bible speaks that bullying is a sin and the bully should repent for his/her wrongdoing and ask the Lord to remove the evil spirit. Please read the chapters and verses that are listed below to help you understand more about bullying according to the Bible so that you will not allow Satan to trick you into joining his evil bullying workshop.

Proverbs 6:16-19; Matthew 5:44-45; Psalms 34:13; Romans 12:19-20; Galatians 5:13-15; I-Peter 3:10 and Ephesians 4:29.

Now that you have read and became familiar with the chapters and verses regarding bullying, share that information and scriptures with others so that they will never consider becoming a bully and not only that, they will know how to witness to people who are actually bullies whether they are in school, church, etc.

I can remember when I was growing up and bullying did exist but it wasn't as severe as bullying is today. Yes, I was bullied (meaning "I dare you to do this", or, "I dare you to do that") by some children in the neighborhood and also at school, at the park, etc. For some reason, I was never afraid of anybody and I have always had the instincts of a lion who is very observative and defensive. For instance, when I was growing up I was very smart, intelligent and beautiful and everyone admired that about me. But there were some girls that lived on the next street from me and we will always meet in the alley to play and I was so lovable until I never thought that any of those girls were jealous of me whether it was my attractiveness, hair, body, smartness, etc. There were times when they would turn on me like a pit bull wanting to fight me and I never could understand the reason why, but they had plenty of sense because they wouldn't challenge me one at a time, they would come in a group (approximately four or five). They would come in the alley where we played, which was near my home and holler out cruel and daring words and make fond of me and daring me to come in the alley or if they caught me at the park or neighborhood store, what they were going to do to me. It hurt my feelings so bad because we would play this day and the next day or week, they want to fight me without giving me a reason. Well, one day I called their bluff, I went to the park along with my cousin and she had my back because she knew that I could handle two at a time. We would fight then be back playing but in today's society, bullying is crucial and illegal and now they believe in killing. To reiterate, there are numerous kinds of bullying such as cyber, social media, etc. Bullying is unethical and God isn't pleased with that satanic behavior.

IV. Burglary

Burglars – there are multiple motivations for engaging in burglary such as: A person may feel that burglary is an easy and quick accessible way of supporting their needs, habits, or wants and desires, instead of working to support them. Additional motivators for burglary are drugs, money, foolishness, and thrill-seeking. However, most burglars usually use a stolen vehicle, or maybe a family member's or a friend's vehicle, when they have planned to carry out a burglary crime. Not only that, some burglars target their prey while walking or just driving a couple blocks away and they usually work alone or together.

What deter burglars from burglarizing specific targets? (1) Close proximity of other people including traffic; those walking nearby; neighbors; people inside the establishment; police officers; lack of escape routes and indicators of increased security such as: Alarms; alarm signs; dog inside; and outdoor cameras or other surveillance equipment. (2) The presence of a loud alarm would cause hot-handed burglars to seek an alternative target altogether. Did you know that professional and rookie burglars have lots of techniques they often use when committing a burglary crime? Some of them are: (1) Enter through open windows, doors, or forcing windows or doors open. They are also known to pick locks or use a key that they had previously acquired to gain entry. (2) They normally cut telephone or alarm wires in advance, (3) the three well-known burglary tools are screwdrivers, crowbars and hammers. Needless to say, once burglars have access to the stolen goods or items, they quickly dispose them for money either to strangers, pawn shops, second-hand dealers, friends and relatives or an exchange for drugs.

V. Hate Crime

<u>Hate means:</u> (1) intense hostility deriving from fear, anger, envious, or sense of injury. (2) Extreme dislike or antipathy (3) to feel strong aversion or intense dislike towards the same or different race.

<u>Crime means:</u> (1) An action or activity that is considered to be evil, shameful or wrong; (2) A violation of the law in which there is injury to the public, or a member of the public and a term in jail or prison, and/or a fine as a possible penalty. (3) An action or omission that constitutes an offense that may be prosecuted by the state and punishable by law.

<u>Hate Crime means:</u> When one race is known to continue intense hostility deriving from fear, jealousy, and envious against another innocent race for no apparent reason that is passed down from generation to generation. Also, a hate crime can include violent action within the same race.

In today's society, according to statistics, African Americans are the main target to be wrongfully murdered throughout this world by the opposite race and they usually escape justice by using weak alibis such as excessive force was needed for self-defense, or the victim had a weapon in which a law was passed to constitute an individual to carry a weapon if he/she so chooses. However, people who hatefully walk around with revenge, bitterness, and envy in their hearts and minds, are vulnerable to commit a hate crime either physically, or in some form of enslavement. It's not all the time that people who commit a hate crime is suffering with a mental-illness. For instance, people can be taught as a child to hate various races, religion, countries, gender, etc., and that negative ungodly teaching becomes <u>rooted</u> in that individual. In addition, jealousy towards another person, whether it's their hair, appearance, skills, gifts, talents, job, car, or home, can cause hatred within another human being and that vicious animosity, feeling, and spirit can escalate into criminal thinking such as vandalizing the victim's property (home); robbing, hi-jacking, theft (meaning property such as a vehicle, equipment, etc.), but most of all, <u>hate crime</u> is usually in the form of vicious or cold-hearted murder.

My sisters and brothers in Christ, it's going to take us (*you and me*), to make a difference in our society by first, learning to love as God loves and learning how to forgive those who misused and abused you. As a child or an adult, a person could have been taught to hate other human beings, but even if hate begins to build up within you, just pray three times a day asking and believing the Lord to remove that evil spirit and thought from your mine and to give you strength to love every one including your enemies. Also, while praying, ask the Lord to diminish all negative thoughts from your mind and fill your heart and mind with love and forgiveness for all mankind. Although you might feel that is a complicated thing to do, just know your flesh can't handle that task alone, and that's why it's imperative to seek God's assistance and power. Now, <u>take the time to meditate on the scriptures following the Ten Commandments in Chapter One, and allow them to explode in your minds, thoughts, and hearts.</u>

VI. Child Abuse

In order for child abuse to occur and to become obsolete, people must be able to recognize the abusive behavior that secretly lives within the hearts and minds. However, sometimes feeling angry and frustrated and don't know where to turn is a sign of abusive behavior within yourself. Of course, I can attest that rearing a child is one of life's greatest challenges and it can easily trigger anger and frustration in the most even tempered. For instance, if you grew up in a household where screaming and shouting or violence was the norm, you may not know any other way to raise your kid. Needless to say, child abuse is a serious crime towards innocent children who didn't ask to be born, but the Lord formed them in the womb of a woman (it took a man's sperm to fertilize the ovary or egg in the female), to reproduce a living being. Let's gain some firm knowledge about child abuse by first knowing its true definition. According to *HelpGuide.org*, child abuse is when a parent or caregiver, whether through action or failing to act, causes injury, death, emotional harm, or risk of serious harm to a child. There are many forms of child maltreatment, including neglect, physical abuse, sexual abuse, exploitation, and emotional abuse. However, most people view child abuse as a physical factor such as broken bones or bruises, but it's far greater than that. Perhaps, neglect and emotional abuse can cause a child to have unfavorable memories and incurable scars in his/her heart and mind for life.

Abused children have a greater chance to recover if help is provided in a timely manner during its early stage. Now, just think for a moment—have you ever thought or realized that a child is a precious gift from the Lord and he's entrusting the parent(s) to rear that child in the appropriate manner such as: Rearing in a positive environment; teaching the child about Christ and how to pray; teaching the child about biblical chapters and events including the principles the Lord established for our daily lives, which are the Ten Commandments? In addition, God appointed parents to be a positive role model for the child and not only that, the Lord entrusted the parent(s) to give the child plenty of tender loving care. On the other hand, the Lord doesn't smile on an abusive person towards a precious child, and the parent(s) must be careful how the helpless and precious child is reared and treated, because the Lord has a purpose for that child's life and you will never know the mission the Lord has for his kingdom through that God-gifted child if he/she is abused and confused. Needless-to say, if the child is experiencing drama, neglect and abuse, those are distractions from the pit of hell to hinder the child from fulfilling God's mission for his/her life and the parent will be held accountable for any abuse or neglect the child may experience.

I often wonder how a person's conscious can allow them to abuse a beautiful and loving, precious handmaiden that God created. Does that abuser really have a heart? It really touches my heart when I see signs of abuse a child is experiencing, or even hear of a child being abused. Compassionately, I tells the Lord how I wish I could take that little angel and raise him/her and give the child plenty of attention, kisses; hugs; tender love and care, while telling the child just how much King Jesus and I love him/her. I must say, on the other hand, there are various reasons why a child experience abuse mainly by parents or a caretaker, but I will only elaborate on several reasons because this topic is really a book of its own, so stay focused and really grasp my explanation and possible solution that will eliminate this crime towards innocent precious and humble children.

First, a parent probably doesn't really know how to rear a child because she/he didn't receive the proper rearing. Therefore, the parent's instinct is to raise the child according to the way she/he was reared, or the way the parent saw other people raise their child. In short terms, the parent probably was abused; hollered at; cursed at, even beaten and called ugly and unpleasant names such as, "a little devil", so that's the only way the individual knows how to raise a child. There's a great possibility that the parent was never told or shown differently, so the parent(s) thinks the child is being reared properly. Another reason for child abuse — possibly the parent or caregiver could be on drugs, in another stage of mind, and has an uncontrollable temper and a low tolerance and maybe abuse the child unintentionally. Although a child can arouse anger by being disobedient; unnecessary crying, acting out of control; disrespect towards the parent and others, etc. — always take a deep breath, calm down, think before you react, then discipline the child out of love and not with force, abuse, and foul language and just be mindful that a child is going through learning stages, which requires the parent to lead, guide, and teach the child right from wrong patiently. In reality, parents have a great responsibility that the Lord is holding them accountable for successfully rearing the child and bringing out the best in him/her through love, respect, affection, and control of temperament.

In conclusion, most parents have animosity toward the male parent during pregnancy or even when the child is born, and often use the child to take out their anger, frustration, hate, and animosity hoping it will get the attention of the mate by abusing an individual he loves, which is his child, while it's in the womb or even when the newborn enters this world. Although the child resembles the other parent that you probably hate the sight of for some apparent reason, God is very displeased when an innocent child is abused just to seek revenge or control from the opposite parent. However, if the other parent sees the child being abused, (if there's any love for the child), the abuse will touch the loving parent's heart and he/she will give in to the abusive parent all for the sake of the child. This kind of abusive behavior is unacceptable in the eye-sight of God and it's also a satanic strategy to gain control of the lovable and caring parent.

Are you aware that child abuse is a double crime, which is legally and spiritually? Therefore, a child abuser will have to answer to the legal system and the Almighty God. Who would want to receive a double dose of discipline? Perhaps, child abuse can easily be avoided by first learning about God's genuine love and how he shares it with every human being. After learning about God's genuine love and how he unselfishly and gracefully shares it with everybody, meditate on it; allow it to absorb in your mind; allow it to rapidly diminish all of the bitterness in your heart, and allow it to embrace your soul. Next, start loving children and people (everyone) the exact way God loves you and me. Just remember, God whispers positive thoughts and actions in our minds, whereas Satan motivates and pressures people to hate, mistreat, lose control, react aggressively without thinking, and he's not a friend that loves you and cares about your well-being. In fact, he's a dirty low-down snake that manipulates people to harm precious children that God has a purpose for their lives and Satan (also known as Lucifer), uses abusers to block that purpose. Today, defeat Satan and his tactics by choosing God's tactics because he's the one who loves and cares for you. If you have abused a child before, make a change now and repent—God is waiting to forgive you for your satanic actions.

Precious, loving, and humbled children need to know that their parent is concern about their well-being and safety. However, an abused child tends to feel alone, unsafe and uncared for and they really don't know what to expect from the parent such as an unexpected whipping; a slap; or an emotional hurt by calling them unpleasant names. Most abused children often experience emotional abuse on a regular basis such as belittling, humiliation, embarrassment, yelling, threatening, and bullying. In addition, *child neglect* is a well-known type of child abuse that fails to provide a child's basic necessities such as, clothing, hygiene, food and even supervision. However, in some cases a parent might become lack in those areas of providing basic needs for a child due to a serious injury, anxiety, untreated depression, alcohol and/or drug abuse. Many physically abusive parents and caregivers insist that their actions are simply forms of discipline—ways to make children learn to behave. However, there's a difference between using <u>physical punishment</u> to discipline and <u>physical abuse</u> as a form of disciplinary action. Please know that the purpose for disciplining children is to teach them right from wrong, and not make them live in fear. Of course, child abuse and neglect occur in all types of families—even in the family that looks happy from the outside—children are often at a much greater risk in certain situations.

Another kind of abuse is *sexual*, which is a hidden type of abuse. However, sexual abuse doesn't always involve body contact. Perhaps, it could be exposing a child to sexual situations or material that is sexually abusive, whether or not touching is involved. Did you know that sexual abuse is normally committed by someone the child knows and should be able to trust—most often close relatives? Girls are not the only one who are at risk. Perhaps, boys and girls suffer from sexual abuse. In fact, sexual abuse of boys may not be underreported due to shame and stigma. Aside from the physical damage that sexual abuse can cause children, the emotional component is powerful and far-reaching. Nevertheless, sexually abused children are tormented by shame and guilt and deep within their hearts and minds they may often feel that they are responsible or somehow brought the ill-treatment upon themselves. This can lead to self-loathing and sexual problems as they grow older—often either excessive promiscuity or an inability to have intimate relations.

Warning signs of *sexual abuse* in children are: (1) trouble walking or sitting, (2) displays knowledge or interest in sexual acts inappropriate to his/her age, or even seductive behavior, (3) doesn't want to change clothes in front of others or participate in physical activities, and (4) runs away from home. There's also warning signs of *physical abuse* that are very noticeable in children and some of them are: (1) Frequent injuries or unexplained bruises, welts, or cuts, (2) injuries appear to have a pattern such as marks from hand or belt (3) shies away from touch, flinches at sudden movements, or seems afraid to go home and (4) wears inappropriate clothing to cover up injuries, such as long-sleeved shirts on hot days. In addition, some warning signs of *child neglect* include: (1) clothes and ill-fitting, filthy, or inappropriate for the weather, (2) hygiene is consistently bad (unbathed, malted and unwashed hair), (3) noticeable body odor, (4) is frequently unsupervised, left alone, or allowed to play in unsafe situations and unpleasant environments; and (5) is frequently late or missing from school.

VII: Domestic Violence

During a domestic violence dispute, likely someone will experience an injury or possibly death. However, there are numerous factors that contribute to domestic violence that you should be aware of and possibly avoid. Whether you know it or not, domestic violence has to do with an unpleasant behavior that is controlling and/or abusive. Although in a relationship, respect is expected from each other, which is always not agreeable. Perhaps, someone in the relationship, whether it's the male or female, is going to feel in control for some apparent reason whether it's taking care of all or more than half of the responsibilities, which includes providing food, paying the rent or mortgage, paying the utility bills, etc. The <u>**roots**</u> of domestic violence and other types of violent relationships are <u>power</u> and <u>control</u>, which are highly linked. For instance, if the man feels the need to dominate the female in any shape or form, whether it's emotional, economic, physical, sexual, or psychological, then it's significantly more likely a relationship will turn violent. On the other hand, it's important to note that abuse is a learned behavior, which in some cases, could have been learned early on in childhood. An abuser may have witnessed domestic violence in the home and perceived that violence was a means of maintaining control in the family unit.

Other factors that cause domestic violence are significant life changes, such as pregnancy or a family member's illness. In these cases, the perpetrator may feel left out or neglected and may seek to regain control over the survivor. In addition, economic down turns such as job loss, housing, foreclosure, or debt can lead to increased violence as well. Regardless of what you are experiencing in life although it can be depressing; cause anxiety; frustration; anger, etc., learn to have control over your thinking and reactions because what satan put in your mind to do—refuse the offer because the Lord don't put no more on you than you can bear and just know that fighting, cursing, assaulting and killing doesn't resolve the problem—it only makes matters worse.

Seven Steps to Avoid Domestic Violence in a Relationship

1) When choosing a mate, choose a person that's compatible to you, or have the same characteristics and values. For example: What are your likes and dislikes; do you attend church? Are you employed or unemployed; how is the prospective mate reared; what are his beliefs; attitude toward children; is the person rowdy, or descent and intelligent.

2) Get an understanding as to what is expected in the relationship; furthermore, just date for several months so you can get to know each other and experience some of the characteristics or values both possesses and to see if they would be favorable or unfavorable; tolerable or intolerable.

3) Use of communication—is the person you are interested in a communicator or non-communicator?

4) After committing yourself to a relationship, both partners should respect each other according to the guidelines agreed upon in the relationship.

5) Whenever there's a disagreement about any situation in a relationship, reframe from arguing, barking, and becoming hostile—just share each other's point-of-view by being intelligent and civilize allowing one to speak at a time. Try to resolve the discrepancy between yourselves and without outside assistance. Take the problem to the Lord and he will surely give you leading and guidance.

6) Both mates must realize that no one has control over the other, and respect plays a major component in the relationship. Do unto others as you will have them to do unto you

according to Luke 6:31 and Matthew 7:12 in the Bible.

7) After dating for several months, both partners should discuss what they think and how they feel about each other, and the expectations in the relationship. (Without an understanding of the expectations, confusion can lead to a domestic violence altercation). Both mates must decide if the dislike(s) would have a bearing on the relationship and depending on the severity of the dislike(s), both partners should decide whether the dislike(s) can be corrected and if they can't be corrected — there's a possibility that at some point-in-time the dislike(s) can lead to an argument, a lack of communication or misunderstanding, anger, unhappiness, emotional disturbance and possibly a violent action well-known as *domestic violence*, which is illegal and can cause an embarrassing reputation for both partners especially if the law enforcement has to resolve the altercation.

Yes, in a relationship there will be disagreements and misunderstandings because we are human beings and we are prone to make errors and no one on this earth is perfect, so what we must learn to do is acknowledge the problem and discuss five possible resolutions for the problem(s) in the relationship. Next, both partners should come to a mutual agreement on the final resolution. However, if both partners can't agree upon the same resolution, then discuss the top *three* resolutions in depth telling **a)** the reason why that resolution was chosen, **b)** discuss the benefits in the resolution and, **c)** will the resolution be a temporary or permanent solution to the problem. From there, I'm confident that both partners will agree on one resolution to bring balance and harmony to the relationship, while closing the door on an opportunity for domestic violence, which is one of Satan's tools to cause harm and change the positive feelings toward one another. Both partners should pray daily for *wisdom* and *strength* because that's what it takes to overpower Satan's tactics in a relationship and in life physically, mentally, emotionally, and spiritually.

Now that I have shared seven critical key pointers with you so that domestic violence will not be a partaker in your relationship, take heed and start implementing them. These pointers can also help you to analyze your relationship and if domestic violence exists, the above key pointers can assist you with enjoying a healthy and romantic relationship by being *acceptable* to change. With that being said, let's discuss in depth several of the seven steps on how to prevent domestic violence in a relationship. *First*, from years of experience, it's advisable to date for several months prior to diving into or being committed to a relationship. That dive is just like not knowing how to swim by splashing and fighting the water hoping not to drown. Although people have their views, opinions, and beliefs about the ages of the two who have each other's interest, some people feel that you shouldn't date a person that's a few years older or younger than you; some people think that you shouldn't date outside your own race; some people feel that you shouldn't date a male or female who is not wealthy or own a nice house and/or car. However, I'm a strong believer that a male or female that's age 18 (if a graduate from high school), shouldn't date any one that's under the age of 17, because more in likely, that individual hasn't graduated from high school and dating occasionally, can be a distraction or a hindrance from that person becoming a high school graduate with honors. On the other hand, usually when someone date a person 10 or more years younger than himself/herself, the older mate (male or female) tends to treat the younger mate like a child by trying to change the individual's lifestyle and take him/her back to the rearing stage and in most cases, the older mate will try to control and instill fear in the younger mate thinking she/he hasn't been taught about the games and lines that are used in society to manipulate.

In conclusion, when dating, expectations from both partners are critical because without an understanding and acceptance of each other's expectations, domestic violence can move swiftly and angrily causing animosity and grief to build up between both mates. In addition to expectations, it's very imperative to communicate effectively while dating or in a relationship. Never allow one another to make assumptions about your thoughts, feelings, or plans. Instead, communicate (talk to each other and be truthful and honest) by expressing your feelings, opinions, desires and plans.

When I meet a young man and he expresses his feelings toward me, the first thing I ask is what are you expecting from me because some men are wanting their fantasy fulfilled with just one time in bed just to say that he's been there and boast about it to his friends. Or, the male might say that he just wants to get to know you better and become friends. There again, I ask him what he expects as friends. Ladies, you really have to be on your p's and q's because all kinds of tricks are out there and never allow yourself to be tricked, used and abused as a sex machine or a sex doll because a friendship should be about caring and being there for each other and not a "bib, bap, bam" and thank you ma'am. Be aware that the main trick a man will use is to take a woman out to eat. Afterwards, he feels that you are automatically his sex doll. Don't' be afraid to get an understanding and ask him what supposed to take place after lunch or dinner unless you are expecting and have in mind that you are gained for having a sexual affair after you've been fed. Perhaps, some men will say, "We will just let nature take its course." No! No! Ladies never allow the man's nature to take its course—you should always be in control of your body and mind and never allow neither one to be disrespected or taken advantage of by no individual. I have experienced that little game on numerous occasions in my life and a man don't like when you are in control of your body because he feels that eating is a woman's weakness and that's why right today, I let a man know upfront that I can pay for my own meal, if he would like because I'm going home after we finish eating unless he wants to walk through the park or store.

VIII. Murder and Mass Murder (which means killing several people in a short length of time, typically in one event)

According to a study at the University of Glasgow, it found a complex relationship between neurodevelopmental problems and psychosocial factors. The study found that 28 percent of multiple killers were believed to suffer from autism spectrum disorder (ASD) and 21 percent had suffered a definite or suspected head injury in the past. However, the lead researcher at the University of Glasgow, stated that it's crucial to note that the study is not trying to suggest that individuals with ASD or previous head trauma are more likely to be serial killers or commit a serious crime. Instead, researchers are suggesting that there may be a subgroup of individuals within these groups who may be more likely to commit serious crimes when exposed to certain psychosocial stressors. (http://www.independent.co.uk/news/science/what)

Seven known reasons to kill or murder and all are unbiblical

(a) *Personal Revenge* - Humans are known to react out of their character when someone whether it's a relative, friend or the unknown, has hurt them in some kind of way such as lying to them; stealing from them or, perhaps, physical abuse. At a moment of anger and mistrust, people tend to lose control of their aggression and feelings. The victim tends to allow the mistreatment to build up within and over power self-control. In any given situation of a person who experience hurt, the first thing comes to mind is revenge. Yes, the victim might say or think, "If I got to hurt, oh! You will too." However, the helpless victim of *hurt and mistrust* allows the mind to decide on whether to kill the other person or inflict some pain on him/her in return. Although it's hard to forgive or not want revenge, we must keep in mind the consequence that one must pay if revenge is done in a violent or criminal way. Regardless of the severity of the situation that might cause personal revenge, remember to always take a deep breath—think twice before you act on your impulses and don't allow Satan to store evil and drastic thoughts in your mind towards another human being who intentionally or unintentionally done you wrong. Yes, I must agree that it's hard to forgive someone who has hurt you, but that's when God's genuine love should overshadow or overpower the thought of revenge. Turn your situation over to the Lord, for vengeance is his *(Romans 12:19)*. When you allow the Lord to handle vengeance, you don't have to worry about legal consequences—just rejoice because victory will be yours. Always remember and be patient because the Lord may not come to our rescue when we want him, but he's <u>always</u> on time.

(b) *Serial Killers* – are human beings that have two different personalities such as sociopathic and psychopathic and usually they don't have a specific group of people they target—they just kill the unknown and the innocent. On the other hand, if a serial killer experienced an unpleasant treatment while growing up such as abuse, then more and likely a serial killer will seek revenge and likely target children to murder. In addition to seeking psychiatric attention, serial killers should pray to the Lord for healing and genuine love. One can prevent being labeled as a serial killer by not allowing your mind to be a breather for Satan to instill those harmful thoughts and feelings in your heart and mind. Without a doubt, our God can heal a hurting and broken heart. Not only that, one of the Ten Commandment says, "Thou shall not kill". Just think about that, when one person is murdered, the murderer must answer to the Lord—but murdering a group of people makes the Lord even more displeased with the action and behavior of the triggerman. Nevertheless, a mental serial killer, without a doubt, must answer to judgment twice (legally and spiritually). No excuse or alibi will be accepted for going on a killing spree because God didn't give you that satanic assignment.

(c) *Mental Illness* – A person with a mental illness still doesn't have approval by God to kill no human being although his/her mentality is highly disturbed. People who are diagnosed with schizophrenia, paranoid psychosis, or any depressive illness, feel threatened and attacked. They are known to kill and will not face legal consequences, instead, they will be confined to a mental institution. A person shouldn't use a mental illness as an excuse to take breath from another human being's body. With sincerity, a mental ill person should ask the Lord for complete healing, and to be made whole, because Satan uses a person with a mental illness as a suspect for violence and crime, which is his dirty work.

d) *Gang Violence* – From my point of view, a gang is a group of people (teenagers, youths, young adults, etc. – no age or race discrimination), which includes a ring leader whose life is committed to violence and crime. Members in a gang feel that selling drugs is quick and fast money and they normally don't have any compassion or love for themselves or other people. Gang members also believe that murdering other people, whether it's beating them down, robbing, burglarizing their home or property, is the right way in life. Usually, a child joins a gang because he/she hasn't been taught the true facts of life; parent(s) shows them no attention; no support; love or concern, so they are very vulnerable to being easily persuaded in the wrong direction. Nevertheless, once a person has formed a gang or has been bullied or persuaded to join a gang, it's very hard for them to change their lifestyle or withdraw from the gang because they have become accustomed to that thuggish culture. I must warn you that gang members too, must answer to God Almighty.

(e) *Political or National Violence* – This is when soldiers of other countries are at war against each other due to political reasoning murdering hundreds and thousands of humans from both sides.

Without a doubt, someone will be held accountable for this unethical action.

(f) *Violence in Various Religions* – People have the freedom to choose what religion they would like to be a part of even though Heaven is not made up of religions or denominations. As a matter of fact, some religions justify killing other human beings for whatever reason they feel that is against their beliefs. Religion will not save you and just know there is only one God, one truth, and only one way to enter Heaven where no violence or religion will separate us for we all will be united as one.

(g) *International Violence* – International violence could possibly be when the government send their armies to other countries to invade for other government power and possibly killing thousands of innocent soldiers. Another international violence is when other countries sell weapons to other countries to ignite a war or to continue the violence that is taking place in their country.

All of the above reasons for killing or murdering one another are unjustifiable and they are also being ignorant and rebellious toward the established principles (Ten Commandments) for our lives. In addition, people need to start thinking before reacting in any given situation and just know that taking someone's life or injuring them is not the <u>root solution</u> for that problem. We must learn to have control over *anger, temperament, emotions,* and learn to communicate with each other without any violent thoughts or intentions. For example, if you hit a driver from behind unintentionally, isn't the first thing both of you do is exit your car to assess any damages done to both vehicles? Next, the driver who hit the other vehicle starts explaining to the other driver what happened—maybe the driver's foot accidently slipped from the brakes. Or, maybe you and the other driver discuss whether to call the police or not for an accident report. Well, that's what should be done in any situation—instead of jumping out the car, allowing your blood pressure to rise and using profanity and being rude and hostile towards the driver who accidently bumped the back of your vehicle. Of course, no one wants their vehicle tapped but just know we are humans and accidents can happen, and we must handle the situation in a loving and godly manner as previously stated and be mindful that violence is not the resolution to the accident—it will only cause more problems and money, such as assault charges and possible confinement to jail—Wow! Satan would really be balling and laughing at how he controlled your behavior and the trouble he has gotten you into so don't allow him to breathe on your territory (meaning your mind and heart) causing you to retaliate violently in which he will not represent you when the time comes to be held accountable for your negative, evil, satanic actions so stay positively focused.

Allow me to elaborate on *workplace* violence, which is also happening right today. From what I've observed and experienced throughout the workforce, the way some supervisors and managers treat an employee in a disrespectful manner can cause violence in the workplace and there are also some supervisors who will promise an employee a promotion or raise just to have the employee perform additional tasks and some just might have been delegated from the supervisor's responsibilities and over a period of time, the promise from the manager or supervisor is never fulfilled—can you imagine how you will feel? Yes, a little hot and angry. Another instance that can cause violence in the workplace is when a supervisor or manager attacks an employee in an unethical manner due to a personal feeling towards the employee. For example, the supervisor or manager probably is jealous because of the way an employee dresses; an employee's intelligence or appearance, so the supervisor or manager start making false claims against the employee and finally termination in which there were no legitimate reason for the termination but the head just wants to flex his/her managerial authority, while not thinking about the responsibilities of the employee and that's the purpose why he/she is working, and now since false termination has occurred, the employee is hurt and angry as well as unemployed for no fault of his/her own. Now, this is where Satan speaks to the employee orchestrating exactly what to do, which is to get revenge. Go back to the workplace and get revenge by shooting anybody including the supervisor or manager who caused the friction.

- STOP THE VIOLENCE-

HOW DOES GOD DEAL WITH THE ISSUE OF MASS MURDER

Jesus said in (Revelation 21:8) — but the fearful, unbelieving, the abominable, <u>murderers</u>, whoremongers, sorcerers, idolaters, and all liars, shall have their part in the lake which burneth with fire and brimstone, and is the second death (eternal home). On the other hand, a murderer answering to the legal system (attorney, judge, jurors, etc.) may be found in "contempt" of court, whereas God is (omniscient) and knows everything even when a person is lying or telling the truth, and he's a fair judge who doesn't need the assistance of an attorney, judge, or jury and his judgment is a done deal.

Regardless of a mental illness (sociopaths, schizo, etc.), the person is capable of understanding the do's and don'ts, the rights and wrongs in life and is also capable of repenting for his/her criminal behavior (murdering, stealing, robbing, etc.). Therefore, the individual will be judged for the crime committed and God will either discipline and/or forgive the human being based on his/her willingness to repent. Needless to say, it's people's nature to feel that a serial killer or a mass murderer's violent actions should be unforgiven and that the sin committed is worse than other sins, but in the eyesight of God, according to the Ten Commandments, a sin is a sin, if it's willfully committed against the Ten Commandments and one sin doesn't carry a special weight of judgment no more than the other sin (except blaspheming against the Holy Ghost). However, forgiveness is available upon repentance and yes, there's hope for any situation.

Here's an illustration of an event in the Bible regarding a serial killer. Pontius Pilate took a man named Barrabbus, who was a serial killer, and Christ (talking about Jesus), to stand before the mob so the people could choose which one was to be released from prison. And as we all know, the crowd chose Barrabbus to be freed who was an insane, violent, sociopath. Not only that, the crowd rallied for Jesus to be crucified. (Rom. 27:11-28). Believe it or not, it is written in the Bible, that convicts can be forgiven for their wrongful actions and receive salvation because the Bible speaks that all have sinned and come short of the glory of God (Romans 3:23). Although sin can become an addiction, which means when a person continues in it, or be forgiven and continues to commit the same sin or a different one, that's a sign of addiction and the individual desperately need deliverance before the addiction becomes uncontrollable. In addition, the Bible does not particularly distinguish between sociopathic evil doers and other evil doers—it's the same fate. The wages of sin is death, according to the Bible, but the gift of God is eternal life through Jesus Christ our Lord and Savior and demon possession doesn't remove one from salvation.

In spite of it all, this is where we as servants of God, step up to the plate and help deter violent behavior and criminal activities. If they don't know right from wrong, then it's our responsibility as Christians working on the battlefield for the Lord, to step in and stop them from doing wrong. Convicts should be repentant of all their sins and they will be forgiven by the Lord who is ruler of this universe. Remember, just because the Lord forgives mercifully and graciously, his *genuine love* is not to be neglected, abused, taken advantage of, or taken for granted. His merciful forgiveness most definitely isn't a justification to commit any crime or harm no human being regardless of their race or background. Just know and be mindful that God will definitely chastise or discipline you for your inappropriate actions. (Some people might label God's disciplinary action as a punishment). Yes, just like teachers and parents discipline their child(ren) for their unethical behavior as a way to properly correct and lead them on the right path and to show love—the Lord will do the same because he loves us unconditionally, cares about our well-beings and wants us to be the best that we can be and to fulfill the mission that he has appointed us. You can ask for forgiveness today.

CHAPTER FIVE

WHAT'S YOUR PURPOSE FOR LIFE ON EARTH

People often wonder why they were born and what's the reason for their birth; why are they here on Earth, or in this world. Well, I can most definitely say that your purpose for being born into this world is not to *misuse* or *abuse* one another; not to rob, steal, and brutally attack one another; most definitely not to be violent or commit criminal acts; and last but not least, your purpose for being born into this world or on this earth, is definitely <u>not to kill or harm</u> your sisters and brothers globally.

There are various reasons why people feel they are on this earth. *First*, they feel that they were born (although they didn't ask to come into this world), to lead a good life and try to make the best of it by pursuing an education, establishing attainable goals; being successful and wealthy. *Secondly*, people feel that they are on Earth to be a duplicate of their parents, through appearance, manners, intelligence, education, etc., and to become in life what their parents are—whether it's a school teacher, preacher, administrator, policeman, drug addict, alcoholic, etc. On the other hand, children that are reared in an unpleasant and unsafe environment tend to grow up wanting the opposite for themselves and their children, which is to live in a better and positive environment and surround themselves and their child(ren) around positive and concise people and places. *Thirdly*, people feel that they are on Earth to be counted in statistics or population. They also feel that they were born in this world for their parents and others to provide for them and support their habits while they walk around pretending to be incompetent, lazy, and no desire to make a decent living for themselves or their child(ren), (if any). *Lastly*, take a brief moment to think back when your mother and father were born, then quickly think back to when you were born. Now, when your mother and father were born, without a doubt, at some point-in-time during their childhood, they probably wondered or asked themselves the same identical question, "Why am I on this earth and what is it that I'm supposed to accomplish in life?" As you know, a child must be taught about all phases of life such as, how to pronounce words; their alphabets; how to count; how to be well-groomed; respect; manners, etc. If they are not properly taught the fundamentals and the true principles of life, then they have no other alternative but to speak words that they hear from others; live like others; and try to be like others, because they haven't been taught properly. With that being said, people grow up to be and live the way they've seen models. However, although some pregnancies were not planned by the couple, to reiterate, no human being was born an "accident", because God formed <u>every</u> human being in the womb of the female for a divine purpose, or reason and it's Almighty who sets the time for birth or deliverance from the female uterus and he makes no mistakes.

Now, let's discover your mission while here on this earth. That is, the mission that God established for your life, while being formed in your mother's womb before you ever entered into this world. I'm sure some people have said, or perhaps, wondered why we must live on Earth instead of going straight to Heaven. Nevertheless, you can possibly think of many reasons why we are born in this world, but just know that every individual has a mission and purpose that the Lord assigned to their lives. (Some people might call it an assignment or, "The reason for being on Earth").

Truthfully, we are in this world to fulfill a spiritual and physical purpose, assignment, or mission and it's misleading to believe any other way. There's absolutely nothing wrong with facing challenges that confront us in our daily lives. However, don't forget the fact that you have a soul that needs nurturing and in order to keep up with your daily physical activities, you must receive Godly guidance for your weary soul. For instance, all humans are composed of three important elements and they are: (1) the body, (2) soul, and (3) mind in which all three of them must be given positive nourishment and encouragement at all times. Let's talk about the physical and spiritual missions for your life, and how to discover them on this earth. First, the physical mission, which some people are knowledgeable of and others have no clue regarding a mission. Of course, at a given time in your life, whether it was during childhood, teen, youth, or as young adults, you thought about what you would like to be when you graduate from high school or when you grow up, so to say. In addition, some of us even set goals and a timeframe to accomplish them.

Setting a goal, or goals, for your life as you mature is the right thing to do. Not only that, always plan to be successful in anything you set out to achieve and always remember to pray continuously to God seeking his *leading* and *guidance* for your physical mission. However, some people, even younger adults, don't know what field or industry they would like to explore in order to fulfill their physical mission. Perhaps, they might start out in a fast-food restaurant, attend college majoring in one field for a year or so, and then change their major to another field. However, these changes can sometime lead to an individual discontinuing his/her education due to the indecisiveness about his/her mission (what in life the person would like to accomplish). I must say that due to the indecisiveness, it can also lead a person into trying something that they might feel is less complicated, less time consuming, less stressful, and less expensive to achieve, which can be dealing in drugs (better known as "get rich quick", fast, easy, and tax-free money). That kind of money also has a price to pay such as injustice, or "pay the time for committing the crime."

Please obtain knowledge of some factors that can help you discover your physical mission. *First,* think about what interests you the most. For instance, do you really enjoy selling? Is it something that requires you to be very active and outgoing? Could it be something that requires you to be seen or heard? Or, perhaps, could it willfully be something that requires hard manual labor, which could be very challenging? *Next,* think about exactly what is it that you enjoy doing and the skills and abilities you possess. *Another thought,* exactly what is your passion—what do you *really* put your heart and love into, while trying to become successful in it? *Last,* but not least, evaluate your strengths and weaknesses—sometimes that can help you understand and accept your physical mission. To illustrate, your strengths might be in writing, sports, dancing, cooking, public speaking, or mathematics, etc. In comparison, your weaknesses might be shyness; can't accept rejections; can't adapt well to changes, etc. However, sometimes the areas that your strengths are in may not be your passion and vice versa—your weaknesses might be your passion. Well, if that should be the case, then start seeking assistance to build your strengths toward your physical mission (or goal) and set your mind to successfully accomplish your mission and keep in mind and often repeat this phrase, *"Anything that my mind can believe and conceive, it will most definitely, without a doubt successfully achieve."* Get this saying down in your inner being, heart and mind, while meditating on it daily. With that being said, the Lord has already planned your success for your physical mission—he reveals it sometimes, but most of all, he wants you to discover it yourself.

In conclusion, regarding your physical mission, *starting today,* let's stop the violence and crimes (robbing, kidnapping, stealing, killing, bribery, conspiracy, etc.), that are overpowering the world by precious, intelligent, and bold human beings. Take time out of your busy schedule to discover and fulfill your physical mission, whether it's in the medical field, retail industry, sales industry, restaurant, banking, legal industry, or political industry. Strive towards honestly earning your living and possessions, while respecting the lives and possessions of your sisters and brothers (meaning siblings, neighbors, people in other countries, states, unknown people, etc.). Starting today, seek *change* and start loving everybody as God loves and that's <u>genuinely</u>.

Now, it's time to become knowledgeable about your spiritual mission. Whether you know it or not, the *main* reason we're on this earth is to grow spiritually and everybody has an assigned, unique mission appointed by God to fulfill. However, our Father continues to send us messages every day in our lives and the key is for us to focus on our spiritual growth. Here is a spiritual concept that can enhance your spiritual and personal growth. Please know that a little forgiveness goes a long way if you are looking for a way to nurture your spiritual growth dramatically because God has given your soul (an instrument) to do so and it's called forgiveness in which the Bible speaks of it. It's imperative that we must learn to forgive, so why not start today and forgive those whom you have animosity towards; those who have mistreated you; those who have lied on you, etc.

Before your birth, the Lord assigned a spiritual mission for every individual's life, which means you have a place in his vineyard to work. There's so much work that needs to be accomplished for the Lord, and that's the reason why everyone has a spiritual mission attached to his or her life. Regardless of your age, you might often wonder exactly what's your purpose for being on Earth. Please know that your reason for being in this world is for a *positive* and *constructive* one and not to indulge in Satan's workshop by inflicting harm and pain to other human beings, committing crime(s), and engaging in violent activities. However, if you haven't already been introduced to your spiritual mission, then continue to pray and seek God through his son, Jesus, for guidance. Nevertheless, you must keep your head up and eyes opened because the Lord may not exactly speak your mission, but show you various things, or situations, that will come together like a puzzle and as a whole, it will reveal your mission. A prime example of how the Lord reveals spiritual missions—throughout life, because of the negligence from my paternal mother and father during my childhood, I have always felt like I was an "accident child", because my mother hardly shared quality time with me and would often ignore me when I gladly saw her and wanted to give her a kiss and hug. In comparison, my paternal father, has always ignored me and only had one conversation with me in life and that was when I was about thirteen or fourteen and my oldest sister showed me exactly who my paternal (or real father was), and at that time he acknowledged that he was my father, although he was dating my mother outside of his marriage, and the only conversation that he had with me at that time was the reason why he was never a father figure to me, which was a very poor and lame excuse. But, praise be to God who blessed me with an angelic grandmother and stepfather who proved my "accidental birth" mentality to be just an illusion, and they gave me indispensable love, rearing, attention, and affection. However, from childhood up to now (as an adult), I have always loved the Lord, prayed and sought his guidance for my life. Nevertheless, during my maturity—love, care, and respect for people have always been my passion. When people hurt, whether I know them or not, I feel their pain and starts praying and crying out to the Lord on their behalf, and if I could physically do anything for them, I happily would.

To make a long story short, in 2010, my children and I begin to experience several storms in our lives and it started with our home being <u>fraudulently</u> foreclosed leaving us having to quickly find shelter, which was a hotel or motel. During that same storm, lightning struck, and I could no longer pay my car note, so I voluntarily returned it to the finance company. In addition, during that same storm, the Lord showed us mercy by granting us a better and more convenient place to live and that was a specific apartment property. It was specific because no other apartment properties that I contacted would house us because of foreclosure regardless of its fraudulency by the mortgagor (bank). This is the place that the Lord ordained for my daughter and I to discover our *spiritual mission*. However, we stopped focusing on the storms and started focusing on the Lord and what he will have us to do for his kingdom. Needless to say, my daughter started pulling out all of her poetry and lyrics, which are very inspirational, that she had written since she was nine years old. They also touched my heart very dearly and motivated my faith. *Next,* we experienced another calamity while keeping our focus on God and praying to his son, King Jesus, which was in February 2013, when a horrible change took place where I was employed. Unfortunately, new management came to the council and decided to restructure the non-profit organization including the staff's roster and their goal was to terminate all existing employees, but several of them who received fraudulent write-ups and verbal warnings managed to quickly seek new employment and successfully escaped fraudulent termination. However, after 11 years of dedicated service, I stayed and allowed the Lord to make the decision for me to get terminated or remain employed and believe it or not, I was the very last one to be terminated and I was so glad and relieved because the dirty work that management was doing towards the existing soldiers was really evil and unethical. In the midst of that storm, my daughter and I kept holding on and remained focused and trusting in God. Although some people saw our storm as a punishment, we accepted it as a *blessing* in the *lesson*. I felt that the Lord chose me and my household as his representatives, so we had to experience some things that Job experienced, and just like Job, our love for the Lord remains the same. Those rugged, raging storms also strengthened our faith, patience, trust, and belief in the Lord, and we knew that the Lord was going to grant us restoration and restitution because years ago we said, "Yes", to his will and purpose for our lives. Whether you know it or not, as his servants—we had to be tried, tested, and encouraged.

The Lord also chose that same special and specific apartment for us to relax and be stable, so that he can reveal our spiritual mission as representatives for him. However, in December 2012, while combing my hair in the mirror, a sweet still voice spoke to me and said to write a book. I looked around knowing I was the only one in the apartment—and I said, "Oh! Lord, you said write?" I told the Lord I love to proof and edit. Again, the voice said, "Write a book and title it God's Genuine Love—Stop The Violence", so I wrote this information down and began praying what the Lord will have me to write about in this book. Because of my willingness and obedience, he has been leading and guiding me every step of this journey. As I got deeper into writing this manuscript, later the Lord spoke and gave me another title and more insight as to what he will have me to share with the people, so the title of this book was revised to "God's Genuine Love-The Root Solution for Violence and Crime". However, I told the Lord that is a very long title for a book but I'm being obedient. Nonetheless, I said all of that, to say this, the Lord allowed me to put the pieces together like a puzzle such as all of the writings (poems and songs) my daughter shared with me and my passion for all of the people in this world. I told my daughter that the Lord has revealed our mission, and it's to partner together to inspire the world by informing the people, "There's hope for any situation", and tell the people not to give up—just put all of their trust and faith in him. Not only that, as his representatives, he wants us to uplift, motivate, encourage, and inspire the people in this world and use our spiritual mission as an avenue to lead people to Christ. Of course, we are two obedient, inspiring individuals going around the city sharing an inspirational table consisting of inspiring self-published books and various items to share encouragement, motivation, and the *root solution for violence and crime*. Well, as you can see, discovering your *spiritual mission* can be revealed <u>at any age, time and place in life</u>. I thank the Lord for assigning me and my household a mission to work in his vineyard because as servants of God we are supposed to motivate, uplift, encourage, and inspire others and lead them to Christ.

Be mindful that when you are working for the Lord by fulfilling the call that's upon your life, you will not be the most loved and popular person by many people. Not only that, this will be the set time by God to reveal your true friends (meaning people who claim to love and support you). Just know that they will either support your spiritual assignment or stray away from you. Not only that, but when you decide to fulfill your spiritual mission, the Lord will start cleaning and removing all the debris and bad branches from your life that could be a hindrance to your destiny that the Lord has prepared for you before you were even born. In addition, you must ask the Lord for strength while traveling your journey because just like the people in the Bible talked bad about God when he only did good by going through the cities healing the sick, giving eyesight to the blind, feeding the hungry—you definitely will be persecuted and called everything but a child of God, but please do not turn back, feel sad or even lonely, because people can't reward you what God has for you, which is supernatural when you obey him and fulfill the mission that he has planned for your life. Hold your head up and keep pushing even if you have to go alone, for God is your leader, guidance, provider, protector and comforter. Just know that our God isn't going to put no more on you than you can bear.

Did you know that when you start living, believing, trusting and working for God, you will feel so great and renewed? As you read your Bible, attend church and give him some praise and worship, your relationship with him will begin to grow and become stronger and you will begin to be a spokesperson for Christ and not being ashamed or afraid who you are standing and speaking for. Of course, you will still experience adversities, trials and tribulations but that's to only strengthen and bless you instead of a punishment or curse. Don't you realize that being a servant for the Lord you will have to endure some things that he endured such as being persecuted, being denied, being negatively talked about, etc.? That's where that genuine love for people comes to play that I have been speaking about throughout this book that we must pattern after. I know in the flesh, it's hard to smile and be really nice to someone whom you know is scanderlizing your name and going around like Satan backstabbing you; belittling you; trying hard to ruin your good reputation, etc. Believe it or not, we still have to love them, but you don't have to love their behavior or actions.

Some people in life experience hard trying times and nothing is going right for them in their life or relationship (where is their God), so they feel that to escape the challenges in life, they will start living for God, not knowing that as a servant of his, you will be tried and sometimes the Lord will allow you to experience a famine in your life where you are down to your last meal and dime and it seems that he will never come to your rescue. Just know that you are being tried and the Lord is testing to see if you will still love and serve him when you don't have anything so be mindful of that—there's no easy way out in this life so choose to serve the one who is the ruler and creator of this universe.

What really amazes me and I really don't understand is when you have been living for God almost all of your life, pay your tithes and sacrifice to help others when you are really experiencing a shortage and is in desperate need of a financial breakthrough—it never comes through so it seems as if you are left all alone to carry this burden with trying to make ends meet. I always ask "where is my God", the miracle worker and ruler of all? On the other hand, there are some people who don't even go to church, pay tithes, nor do they take the time to pick up a Bible and probably never thank God for waking them up to live to see another day and got their health and strength. Seems like they're the ones who get blessed with finance and more and if you know them, you dare not ask them for a penny or a dime because they will look at you as if they deserve it and have worked hard for it and that they are God's favorite. Well, even though I don't understand why some non-believers are blessed before some believers and tithers, I'm still going to keep loving and trusting in God because the believers' blessing is far greater than the non-believers.

CHAPTER VI

RECAP: GOD'S GENUINE LOVE – THE ROOT SOLUTION FOR VIOLENCE AND CRIME

Criminal activities and violence come in many shapes, forms, and fashion. Let's discuss briefly <u>several</u> of them, keeping in mind that these are evil spirits that are *persuading, convincing, incubating, and controlling* the minds and actions of human beings. It's imperative that everybody learn, implement and exhibit *God's genuine love* and make a difference in your life and the lives of others by overpowering the satanic spirits of <u>violence</u> and <u>crime</u>. The Lord said that we have power over Satan, so let's reverse his tactics and give the Lord the respect, obedience, thanks and appreciation that he well deserves and is worthy of. Now, the *first* criminal activity to be briefly discussed is hate crime.

Hate Crime: This is another serious unethical act that is very displeasing to God. In fact, this human behavioral activity has been in existence for centuries and has begun to escalate rapidly and globally, and perhaps, has gotten out of control in this world. Although hatred is more of a *rooted, cancerous, demonic tactic* that was molded into the lives of individuals from their parents, ancestors, pastor, friends, peer pressure, etc., it makes individuals kill other people, <u>mainly</u> those of a different race or skin color. Of course, Satan is the ring leader of this crime and as you may or may not know, he was the most beautiful angel in Heaven trying to form his own clique, so the Lord dismissed him. Without a doubt, that's Satan's life and job to deceive people and use them to perform his harmful and unclean assignments. If people whose heart is rooted with hatred, would take the time to think and analyze their behavior, which has grown cancerous (meaning the hating spirit has circulated throughout the body starting from the mind; to the thoughts; to the heart; then transformed into action), they would come to their senses and realize that Satan has them confused, brainwashed, blinded, and has control over their minds and hearts. Yes, most of the opposite race was taught hatred towards African Americans, but as an individual matures, he/she should take the time to ask him or herself, "Exactly what has the opposite race, or sex done to me personally to instill animosity and hatred within me?" I often thinks about how our race are constantly being treated right today and I often thinks and asked myself, "Could it be that our ancestors' slave masters and those of today, envied the God-gifted talents, skills, and abilities that the African Americans are blessed with, which could have possibly molded hatred into the opposite race who were slave masters for generation after generation?" Why another race wasn't slaves?

The *second* crime to be reiterated is aggravated assault.

Aggravated Assault: People assault others for various reasons and I don't understand why a large percentage of the crimes being committed are against our own African American race. I have not yet discovered why there's so much animosity between our own race. Exactly, why are African Americans so deeply at war with one another? *In short terms (Black on Black) crimes. However, from my research on* past history, *I can't find any historical documentation where our black ancestors hung, drugged, slaved, raped, or beat one another (on their own), or because of hate, envy or jealousy. In contrast, from my research, blacks picked cotton together for the opposite race as a tool for survival and family provision. I have yet to discover in the past era where blacks fought against each other on their own. Instead, they worked together and loved one another. So now, my question is to the African American generations of today and the generations to come — who instilled in your hearts and minds to assault, hate, and have animosity towards your own beautiful, blessed and valuable race? Exactly "Who, Why, or What", causes you to be enemies with your own African American race? Take a moment to think seriously and strongly, is it the color race who's passing gun laws to make it really simple and accessible to assault another innocent person of color? Perhaps, is it your own race who is rapidly building private prisons everywhere to incarcerate the blacks as a form of making money?* <u>Just stop and think hard!</u> Do that mean your African American race is <u>valuable</u>? Have you ever thought about exactly why a male or female of <u>your own</u> race is chosen as a victim to assault or kill? Have you ever thought of an answer to these questions? Could it possibly be that an African American chooses the same race to harm, assault, and injure because the justice or court system consequences are not as *harsh, cruel and punishable*? Well, just take a minute to compare some past and present crimes where a "man of color" harmed a person of the opposite race. Study the *cruel* and injustice punishment that the court system decides for a "man of color" would receive, such as the *death penalty; life without parole*, or possibly be *murdered* in prison and the false reporting would state that "man of color" hung himself or committed suicide.

Now, that you have paused and thought this negative plot of satanic spirits over, has your understanding about the comparison of assaulting one of your own verses assaulting the opposite race *dawned* on you yet, as to what's going on in our society and exactly who's behind and supports black on black crime? Wake up! Wake up! African Americans, it's time to realize how valuable your race is and that's why the system is designed to give *black on black* crime a lesser and lighter criminal punishment. *Just know that I'm not justifying or encouraging any one to engage in any crime regardless of your race, I'm only trying to differentiate the punishments given when an African American harm one of his own vs harming one of the opposite races.* It's imperative that <u>ALL races</u> come together in love and stop the violence. Although our skin colors are different, our blood will always be the same color (red) and that's the way the "Supreme Ruler" created it and that speaks for itself.

People, please realize that assault, whether it's aggravated or simple, is the trick of the enemy (Satan) to use you to commit a crime or assault someone whether it's in a relationship or publicly. Choose *today* to <u>think</u> before you react in any given situation and remember that Satan is not your friend and he's using you to do his dirty low-down work. Not only that, he'll get you in trouble and will not be in the courtroom to help defend your satanic actions so that the judge and/or jury won't hold you accountable. Honestly and truthfully, Satan really doesn't know you any more once he has gotten you in trouble with our God and the legal system, and once the sentencing for the crime committed has been served, old Satan will pay another visitation to give you another satanic assignment to carry out for his glory. Don't be his evil elf (a weak-minded busybody) a second time. My advice is to *start* focusing on the one whom some of you never recognize or respect, but always prayerfully call on in the time of trouble and that's God Almighty, for he's definitely a trustworthy, dependable, and a kind friend who will never leave you alone, nor will he steer you in the wrong direction. Believe me! God loves you so much until sometimes he will show you favor during your court appearance, so why not show him the love and respect that he well deserves? In reiteration, I'm addressing *women and men of color* because of the *high crime rate* being reported among our own race and out of love and concern, I'm kindly pleading and asking *everyone to come together as one* and make a start in decreasing and ceasing the violence and crime throughout the world, which includes ALL races, countries, states, cities, etc. Men and women of color, let's choose today to stop the violence among ourselves and be that positive role model for the <u>"now" and upcoming generation</u>. Also, let's choose today to make a change by learning and <u>incorporating </u>God's *genuine love* in your lives and allow it to replace any animosity in your hearts. Dr. Martin Luther King's dream reflected that everybody of every race, sex, and nationality come together as one and love as one family and every human being regardless of the race, must realize that our races may be different, but the blood in our bodies are one color and that's *red* regardless of the blood type, so that should say a lot about *everybody* loving each other and getting alone because there's only one heaven and God loves all of his creations. If he had favorites, then he would have made our *blood color differently*. Now, think about that for a moment and see the true picture of God's "genuine love" for us. Although Dr. Martin Luther King, Jr. is deceased, his dream for <u>all people</u> lives on, and I'm still an advocate for his dream being fulfilled today. We must realize that our mighty true friend and leader is our Father who sits high on the throne and sees every single action that's taken against our sisters and brothers (known and the unknown) in this world. In addition, Dr. Martin Luther King disapproved of violence and crime to the fullest. Not only that, everybody must realize that assaulting another individual don't prove anything other than you do not have <u>love for yourself</u> because if you did, your heart and conscious would forbid you to inflict harm or injury to another human being. So, starting *today*, let's put forth the effort to stop the violence and crime by sharing Godly knowledge with other people in this world. (Let's share and spread the good news about our Creator and his attributes).

Let's gain insight about <u>three</u> other types of <u>criminal assaults</u> that are unconstitutional and against the principles set forth for us in the Bible. *First,* rape and sexual assault—no one should ever impose themselves on another human being forcefully and without permission from that person. Raping or sexually assaulting an individual can cause damage to an individual emotionally, physically and mentally. *Rape and sexual assault* can change an individual's self-esteem, confidence, trust and feelings towards others. *Secondly,* simple assault—less injury or harm is inflicted on the victim than aggravated assault, but it's still a satanic tactic from the pit of hell (satan) and it should be avoided by asking yourself, "Will God approve of this action?" And what will be the legal and spiritual consequences of the crime that satan is instilling in my mind to commit? *Thirdly,* assault with intent to rob is a horrible act instigated by Satan because God does not instill violent behaviors and criminal actions in nobody's mind and heart, so Satan has to bear the burden that he creates. Again, this crime happens within the majority (black race), which is very devastating and cruel. Why injure someone who is innocent and has worked hard for his/her possession? Take a moment to think about that. Doesn't that sound like a coward or a person who doesn't have love for himself or anyone else, and is too lazy to work for whatever it is that a person inflicts harm on another individual for? *Stop the Violence!!*

Third crime to be reiterated is domestic violence.

Domestic Violence: Domestic violence is happening throughout the world and in reality, the partners are in a dispute over <u>power</u> and <u>control.</u> Perhaps, domestic violence can escalate into a more serious crime such as assault or possibly death, which can be caused by many factors such as materialistic items, verbal disagreements, income level, educational level, etc. and drugs and alcohol are most definitely factors of domestic violence. Normally, a person's attitude and behavior changes rapidly when drugs and/or alcohol is in their blood stream causing them to become loud, hostile, abrupt, aggressive, violent, and stronger. Sometimes an intoxicated person will start an argument using profanity with slurs and looking very weird and ugly. On the other hand, domestic violence can occur without any drug or alcohol present in a person's blood stream and it can also be a dispute over the proper way to rear a child(ren).

For instance, in a relationship, usually the two individuals could have been reared differently, therefore having indifferences about how to rear their child(ren). The female probably was reared in a Christian environment where there was no smoking, drinking, profanity; watching unpleasant movies on television, and no unpleasant music being played in the household—so that's the pattern she would like to rear the child(ren). In contrast, the male probably drinks; listen to gangster music; loves violent movies and wears his clothes in an unattractive and disrespectful way (pants hanging off his rear end, and underwear or split being revealed to the public), which is showing no respect for himself, the child(ren), or the relationship. These indifferences most definitely can cause a family feud, which can escalate into a domestic violence altercation because the male probably feels that he has as much control and power over the child and the relationship, whereas the mother may also feel the same maybe because one of them pays more bills in the house; maybe only one person is working in the house, or it's a norm for the man to feel that he's the head and has total control whether he is or isn't providing or supporting the family. Please read and meditate on the following scriptures daily and allow them to dwell in your memory box and spirit regarding a person who indulges in domestic violence. Proverbs 28:17 — *States that a man that doeth violence to the blood of any person shall flee to the pit.*

Zephaniah-1:9 states, "In the same day also will I punish all those that leap on the threshold, which fill their masters' houses with violence and deceit."

Psalms-37:9 states, "For evil doers shall be cut off: but those that wait upon the Lord, they shall inherit the earth."

I have experienced several past domestic violence altercations when I was younger and dating so that's why I can share some valuable guidance with you so that domestic violence can be avoided because it's embarrassing, hurtful and it tends to affect the mind, feelings and emotions. To also help avoid a domestic violence altercation, both individuals must understand and realize you have parents and I don't think nobody's parent(s) (speaking of the male and female) will give permission to disrespect, hurt or assault their child. To illustrate, in my past relationship, the main ingredient that was very unpleasant or hot and spicy was the male wanting control over me, meaning in short terms, he wants to play the father's role and put me on a "can't punishment" such as, "you can't buy this or that", you can't go here or there", you can't do this or that", and calls himself trying to physically fight me, which is an absolute "no" "no" and a highly misunderstanding because I would always tell the male that we are two individuals and my parents <u>didn't give you permission</u> to raise me because all of the rearing has been done, and I'm not going to put my hands on you when there's a mishap and I pray that you don't put your hands on me when you can't <u>control</u> or instill fear in me. This is also where the seven steps that were previously mentioned regarding how to avoid domestic violence in a relationship also should be implemented and understood by both mates because there are some women who are aggressive and have the same tendency to want control over a male and physically harm him as well.

My sisters and brothers please realize and understand that fussing, fighting and cursing don't resolve anything—it only shows that neither of you are mature; intelligent; have respect about yourselves; have control over your temper, feelings and emotions. When you feel that you are angry or upset about something, just take three deep breaths and call on the name of Jesus and I'm confident that will calm you down because it's the flesh that we are dealing with and it is sometimes hard to control on our own. Just be mindful that domestic violence is of Satan and he never wants anyone happy or their relationship to be happy so he's busy at all times trying to stir "witch brew" and have you growling and hating one another—yes Satan gets a thrill out of all of that because he knows once he turn you against each other, you have given him the keys to your vehicle (meaning mind and temperament) to drive the situation down any road he chooses such as have you assaulting or perhaps killing one another; breaking up and departing; have you taking your anger and frustration out on your children, boss, co-workers, etc. Never leave a door open for Satan to take control over your mind, or anybody the Lord blesses you with such as your mother, father, sister, brother, mate, etc. Satan doesn't care and if you allow him to control your temper and behavior, he will not decline the offer so stay focused on King Jesus.

POLITICAL LEADERSHIP

The system in this world is made up of a group of politicians who are elected or appointed and trusted to have the interest of life and freedom of living. Every group or body of representatives play a diverse role in governing our state and country. Politicians in political offices such as the senate, congress, legislature, governor, etc. possess power and authority within their jurisdiction to make executive decisions such as create laws, pass laws, create amendments, veto bills, etc. Needless to say, Congress and the President are the two most powerful authorities in political leadership. For those of you who don't know, Congress power comes from the Constitution and is formed by the House of Representatives and Senates. However, the Constitution of the U.S. of America is the *Supreme Law* of the United States. It's the source of all government powers, and it also provides important limitations on the government that protect the fundamental rights of the U.S. citizens. On the other hand, Congress is responsible for making new laws and changing existing laws. In addition, Congress is also empowered to enact laws deemed "necessary and proper" for execution of the powers given to any part of the government under the Constitution. Congress also has the sole power to declare war. (www.whitehouse.gov)

With that being said, everybody—meaning you and me, must take a stand *now* and put forth the effort to stop the violence in this world. Everybody has a part in eliminating violence and crime in our cities, neighborhoods, country and state. As far as making executive decisions on the citizens' behalf when it comes to doing business with other countries, the political officers must keep their promises, obligations and be honest and trustworthy. Political officials should also never be dishonest with other countries because that could cause a negative impact on the citizens.

Right today, the Lord is still working *miracles* and our former United States President, Mr. Barack Obama (2009-2017), whom in my opinion and belief, was appointed by God to fulfill the mission that he has for our country and all the citizens therein. Yes, he's a miracle, just take a look at all of the past presidents—there's not one that was a "man of color." However, some of the assignments that I'm confident that the Lord wanted our former United States President to fulfill were: (1) to obey his soft still voice informing him on how to bless everyone especially those who are living in poverty. Not only that, I sincerely believe that the Lord chose our humbled former president (2) to help break the destructive, nonchalant spirit of greed, (3) to bring peace among all countries and restore America back to the land that it was known for especially honoring and acknowledging the one and only God by having prayers in the schools, for one, and most importantly, (4) boldly lead this country according to God's Holy word which is the Bible, and not worry about the consequences because enemies and satanic spirits behind the scene can only do what God allows and no weapon formed against a servant of God will prosper (Isaiah 54:17), and another powerful scripture is, "Greater is he that is within *you* (former president) is greater than he that is in the world." (I-John 4:4) *Secondly,* as we all know, all presidential candidates will make promises during election time about what their plans are for the citizens of the United States.

As for any upcoming United States President, let's first realize that he/she is flesh and blood just like we are, but we elect each one only entrusting that they will be fair, honest, and look out for the well-being of all human beings regardless of race, gender, or religion. However, it never fails that once the elected President takes office, sometimes he starts experiencing amnesia forgetting all of the positive promises he made to the people (possibly some fulfilled and other promises forgotten). Although the citizens don't know the nominees personally; their character; or moral values—normally the vote is based on what the media is saying along with what each candidate is promising the citizens. However, after exercising your right to vote, repetitively, it seems as if the wrong candidate was elected because of his action towards the promises stated during election time. Here's some advice to the other elected and appointed parties in political leadership, choose TODAY to stop indulging and instigating dishonesty and harmful acts toward our neighboring countries causing them to become our enemies and possibly leading to war. You (Congress), has the authority to "Stop the Violence" (war, terror, bribery, conspiracy, etc.), that is going on in this world. Allow God's genuine love to enter into your hearts and look out for the well-being of <u>all</u> citizens.

Let's briefly elaborate on the highest crime rate in the world which is *murder*. Numerous of innocent lives are being destroyed through war and according to the Bible, which is stated in one of the Ten Commandments (Thou shall not kill). Perhaps, only political leadership has the authority and executive decisions to plan and execute war. Just imagine how the world would be if there's no war and all countries are implementing God's genuine love among each other. We really wouldn't need political leadership. Sounds impossible? Well, *with God all things are possible*, and we, as citizens, must boldly take a stand and stop crying, moaning and groaning; pointing fingers, and criticizing political leadership about what's happening in the world. To reiterate, yes, the majority of them promise what they are going to do for the citizens as a scam to get your vote, then when some of the political candidates are appointed in office, their action is totally different from their words of mouth or promises.

Murder: According to the Holy Bible, murder is unacceptable to the creator, God Almighty. To the president and elected officials, you all are the body that the citizens elected, depend upon, believe in, and trust to operate the states, nations, countries, etc., in a fair, honest and trustworthy manner. Not only that, the citizens are holding each of the elected officials (government, senators, house of representatives, etc.) accountable for their behavior, actions, and character towards the country they have been elected to governed and keep peace. Nevertheless, the citizens in this world are holding the politicians accountable for making a dramatic change and to make peace with other countries. However, with the assistance of learning about "God's genuine love and implementing it in their daily lives, can teach and motivate political leaders on how to have love for every human being. Additionally, God's genuine love will also teach political officials how to have peace with other states and countries as well. Most importantly, political officials having knowledge and implementation of God's genuine love will have a <u>positive effect</u> on murder, which is one of the highest statistical crime in the world. No more will our army of innocent males and females will have to go to war ("to kill" or, "to be killed"), because of a disagreement or discrepancy caused by elected political officials, then it is reported to the public that the Army is fighting to protect our country. Exactly, what was done behind the citizens' back to ignite this flame? Murder (war), is *not* the <u>answer or solution</u> to any disagreements, problems, misunderstandings, or perhaps, fighting for <u>power</u> or <u>control</u> over something that is supposedly valuable.

As authoritative leaders of our countries and states, which makes up the world, choose this day to agree upon a *change, for love* towards one another, and peace. All of us as citizens must make a *change* as well to stop the breath of innocent and precious people being taken from their bodies either by being a victim of murder or a murderer. A strong solution to "decrease or cease" the murder rate is to gain the knowledge of "God's genuine love" and exercise it in your daily living and allow it to become <u>rooted</u> within your hearts and minds. Be informed that God is the *only* one who can help you make a positive change in your thinking and feelings toward one another and remove all negative, evil and satanic thoughts from your minds and hearts and allow the Lord to replenish them with love and not the thought of taking someone's life. Think and pray before you react because once a life is taken, you can't restore it, (only the master can) and remember, murder is against the principles of God (Ten Commandments).

People, please consider my suggestion regarding "Change". In order to make this world a better place to live and fulfill your two missions (spiritual and physical), we (meaning every human being), must start utilizing the power that the Lord has given us by putting him first, uniting as one, and boldly take a stand for what we are wanting, which is *change*. Next, as far as elected officials to govern or play the role of the middle man on the citizens' behalf, let's start telling our Father in advance the values that we seek to oversee our well-beings as citizens. Better yet, if we would come together as one, utilize our voice and power; and most importantly, learn to exercise the information from every chapter that is shared in this book, we really wouldn't have to depend on political leadership. With God as our leader and guidance, CHANGE in this world is possible and he can use us to make it happen. As believers in Christ, let's stop allowing the saber tooth powerless to have power over us and our daily living.

Satan has always felt, or perhaps, wanted to be the ruler of this universe, but he isn't the one. Just know that Satan has to receive permission from God and he only allowed Lucifer a limited amount of power and time to roam to and fro seeking whom he can devour. I kindly ask and pray that you don't become a victim for carrying out Satan's satanic plots toward God's beautiful and precious creations, speaking of human beings who have breath in their bodies and were created for a purpose, which is to carry out an assigned mission for God our creator. Don't be a hater like Satan because he has nothing positive and rewarding to offer you. Some people don't know very much about Satan or that he even exists so let me give you a small introduction of this satanic spirit. The Bible tells us that Satan was the most beautiful angel but he got kicked out of heaven because he was trying to form his own click so that should show and tell you that he's a lunatic. Who in the world would trade a place of peace to form your own weak click and don't have the power to offer his click what God shared with him. Since Satan has been booted out from heaven all he has ever done was roam to and fro seeking more lunatics like him and persuade them to do his dirty work so that they will live eternally in his fiery kingdom because his pit doesn't compare to the palace or mansion God has prepared for us after our labor for him down here on Earth. Today, tell Satan you chose to live and work for your creator who has power over him and the universe.

In addition to that, let me tell you more about Satan, the one who even attempted God and told him what he would award him with if he would do what Satan commanded him to do. Isn't that beast stupid and very confused? Satan is jealous of God because he is the creator and ruler of the universe and has all power in his hands. Perhaps, Satan wants to be something that he will never be and that is the most powerful ruler of the world and since he can't have that kind of authority and is no longer in heaven, he just keeps up devilish altercations and conversations with human beings trying to win them over from God. Yes, he's still forming his own click against God down here on Earth and that's why he controls weak-minded peoples' minds telling them wrong actions to take towards other individuals. Take a moment to think, exactly what does Satan has to offer you when you obey his voice? Exactly what good reward will you receive from Satan? Is he the one who touches you with a finger of love allowing you to rise to live and see a brand new day? Is it Satan who protects you from danger seen and unseen? Is it Satan who heals your body when the doctors have given up on you and say there's no cure for what you are experiencing? Is it Satan who supply your every need and blesses you with a job to survive in this mean world? The answer to <u>all</u> of these questions is "No, it's not Satan", but it is our gracious and merciful Father, King Jesus who does all of those great things for us, so choose today to stop being confused and brainwashed by Satan and live, thank and glorify our creator.

BLACK LIVES MATTER

First, I would like to highly commend the person(s) who founded this great and awesome movement to march and protest for justice for hateful and criminal acts against our innocent black race. With God all things are possible and now some justice is being acknowledged and granted by higher authorities for the brutality against African Americans from the envious and hateful Caucasians on the police force around the country and states. I must say, protesters, keep up the representation for the African American race whose lives are very gifted, precious and valuable. Continue to stand up and seek justice for our brothers and sisters (African American race) when hatred has ended their lives in cold-hearted murder from the opposite race for no legitimate reason.

Officer Friendly is known as a true and trustworthy police officer. During the 60's and 70's, I can remember when these officers, would visit the schools to make sure the children are safe and receiving a quality education. *Officer Friendly* would also visit the neighborhoods and get acquainted with everybody including children and making sure their environment was safe. They would also shake your hand and speak positive motivation to every child. Yes, I must say, I do remember some Caucasian *Officers Friendly*, but what happened to both Officer *Friendly* races over the years? I don't know. However, I must say that there is still one well-known *Officer Friendly* who still exists today and maintain that same passion; interest of the children's well-being, safety, and their education. Not only that, in his spare time, he visits the schools to check on the children's progress and grades, and at all times commending and motivating those whose learning performance is on point and encouraging, motivating and rewarding those who shows no interest in an education but reverse their behavior and start making progress in their learning and testing. Not only that, *Officer Friendly* realizes that this generation of young children and the generation to come are our future doctors, nurses, lawyers, police officers and possibly the next president of the United States. This *Officer Friendly* who has been on the city of Jackson police force for 15 plus years and not only does he has a passion and heart for the younger generation, but also has a concern and passion for everyone in this world, just like myself.

As I was explaining the "Root Solution" Movement to Officer Friendly, he brought to my attention another side of *"Black Lives Matter"* that fits really well with "God's Genuine Love-The Root Solution for Violence and Crime". He said that the "Black Lives Matter" Movement should take in consideration that murdering <u>our own race</u> **isn't ok or justifiable** and that violent behaviors shouldn't be ignored. *Officer Friendly* also gave me some insight on the different crimes and killings that he had to investigate, and it's so sad for our race to really be enemies among ourselves for no apparent reason, and also how African Americans choose our own race to take out their anger and frustration for whatever reason. Of course, *Officer Friendly* feels pain in his heart for the criminals and victims *just like I do*. Well, I have a *solution* that I highly feel that the Black Lives Matter Movement should implement <u>in addition</u> to the "Root Solution-No More Bandages". First, Black Lives Matter protesters and supporters should find a place to meet, pray, then take about five minutes to open their hearts and minds to have a passion for the African Americans who are murdering each other. Yes, "black lives do matter" among our own race. Now, take a moment to think just how powerful those three words are (Black Lives Matter) and allow your mentality to change from just one angle or side (Blacks vs Caucasians) to both sides (Blacks vs Blacks). For instance, have you noticed that protesters or the *movement* don't get aroused, irritated, frustrated, or march for justice until a Caucasian police officer murder one of our valuable *Black* lives? Just to reiterate, black lives does matter among our black race as well. Valuable lives are being gunned down by our own race viciously and angrily such as, a black sister or brother might stare at you without a smile; racing for a park place with another black sister or brother, or maybe a man or woman of color driver might pull out in front of you while driving. Additional illegitimate reasons are an argument, robbery; assault, etc. Just really dumbfounded reasons why we are losing our precious black lives over. My brothers and sisters, it's imperative that we come together and start changing our *mentality* and realize that God Almighty has given us the power to control whatever we (African Americans) desire. (Luke 10:19 and II-Timothy 1:17).

I'm pleading that we take a different approach for the murdering (crime) that is rapidly taking place among our valuable race. Don't overlook or ignore the fact that we are assaulting and killing one another and it's **not ok**, although the legal system designed it to be, by passing gun laws and other snares that were plotted for the African American race. Do you ever hear of Caucasians gunning down or assaulting, robbing, and stealing from one another? We hear little to none publicly and the statistics are very low, and the media keeps it undercover. Sometimes when a Caucasian commits a crime, the media will not show a picture only keeping the viewers in suspense and that's how we are highly confident that the suspect or criminal is possibly a Caucasian. Last, but not least, to prove and introduce the Black Lives Matters Movement to our African American citizens as well, let's march to share the *"Root Solution-No More Bandages"* with them and that's "God's Genuine Love — The Root Solution for Violence and Crime", and allow God to deliver justice by converting the criminals and strengthen the victims and their families.

The **Root Solution** for violence and crime is to become knowledgeable about God's genuine love and exercising his pattern of love in your lives and sharing it with others regardless of race, position, gender, etc. However, the bandages are the "so-called" solutions to violence and crime that political leaders and other authorities plan and implement and as everyone can see, the solutions rapidly increase violence and crime. Allow me to share with you <u>four</u> great examples of bandages for violence and crime. *First*, what's happening in the world since carrying a gun law was passed? An increase in innocent "blacks" being gunned down by the so-called "Serve & Protect" Caucasian police officers and the majority of the deceased lives were unarmed and the African Americans who were licensed to carry a gun according to videos—never attempted to display a weapon when they were approached by a uniformed police officer. Therefore, passing a gun law is considered a *bandage* because of injustice of the court authorities. *Second* bandage pertaining to violence and crime is the building of more private prisons to incarcerate—guess who for monetary purposes? *Third* bandage claims that more violence and crime are due to the lack of poverty (meaning lack of education and no jobs, or low-paying jobs) and the so-call solution that political leaders passed by law is to increase minimum wages; employers are to provide benefits to all full-time employees; grant money is available to everyone who wants to attend college or further their education—just to name several bandages, which are better known as *patching* the problems instead of analyzing them from the **root**, then work out the kinks.

Last, but not least, the *fourth* bandage, which is the love and dependency on the government. For decades the government has spoiled young Americans (mainly females) by being lenient in job seeking; having no motivation to want an education or to work, and that's why for decades young females would have numerous children because the government would pay for housing (HUD), food (EBT/food stamps), and give the female a check for each child in the household. Truthfully, government assistance should be designed to assist those who have experienced a crisis; those who are unable to work due to a disability; those who once had a job, but experienced a hardship such as a lay-off, termination, illness, etc. All of this free service from the government to able-body individuals who have the opportunity to earn an education and seek employment to handle responsibilities is only a bandage and teaser. For instance, today, the government is implementing new laws which states that welfare recipients are to seek employment and work at least "X" number of hours in order to continue receiving free government assistance. Do you agree that being self-sufficient should have been enforced by the government decades ago for those who are able to work and just too *trifling*? From my point of view, the government bandage (free service to the able-bodies) has really created an enormous monster for increasing violence and crime. To illustrate, people who have been living off government assistance are spoiled, and they aren't going to accept the change very easily of having to work; go back to school to continue their education, or to become educated. Needless to say, since government recipients are so use to an easy life—they are unlikely to accept change with a smile, but with anger, which will cause them to become violent and commit crimes such as stealing and robbing as a mean for survival. The root solution should have been implemented decades ago to those who chose not to go to school or finish school, or probably refused to apply for employment or declined the offer for employment.

A perfect illustration of *bandaging* a serious problem that affects all drivers and their vehicles are the raggedy, hilly, pothole streets in which some gets their bandage now and other areas gets their bandage (meaning patched with black tar) when it's near election time again. Please realize that this serious problem with the streets in the capital city is in no way a reflection of the present mayor, but it's the reflection of the promise from former mayors to get to the root of the problem that's causing the streets in some areas to deteriorate and discover a root solution. However, I must say that the city of Jackson citizens have been living with serious street problems for ages. Now we have an honest, caring and trustworthy mayor who is working hard to make improvements to the capital's city streets. No doubt! Citizens' vehicle's tires and rims receive damages from the streets that are severely problematic and we still have to pay privilege taxes to ride on them. Just take a look at your renewal card that is mailed to you when you purchase or renew your tag and you will see the break down cost for each category that we are paying taxes for pertaining to our streets in the capital city. To reiterate, yes, the liable department will have the potholes in the streets bandaged (patched with black tar) instead of discovering the <u>main</u> cause of the street's deterioration and seek a <u>root solution</u> because a bandage (black tar) is temporary, which causes the problem to re-occur. In contrast, time, money, and service are being wasted on incompetent solutions for violence and crime by authorities within. Politicians, leaders, mayors, etc., have all tried their so-called solutions for violence and crime and most of their solutions have been bandages, patches, or failures for decades. Now, this is a new era and it's time to try another solution, which is the *cure* for violence and crime because it will start from the roots of these two satanic, cancerous tactics that have been released from the pit of hell and the *root solution* has all the ingredients needed to <u>cure</u> and <u>destroy</u> these two demons (violence and crime). Unfortunately, we must take a stand and unite together with our war clothes on (meaning the whole armor of God) and get started on this journey to victory over violence and crime. Just know that violence and crime most definitely *will not* deteriorate on its own and for years and decades we have seen that higher authorities don't have the necessary tools, knowledge and effective strategies to conquer the demons nor have they discovered the *root solution* for them (violence and crime). Just take a moment to think and think hard and fast. Of course, the information and strategies shared in this book <u>is the cure</u> for violence and crime, so are you just going to ignore this root solution and continue to point fingers at whomever you want to fault or blame for the violence and crime that is terrorizing our cities, states, and countries by the seconds, minutes, hours and days? Are you going to continue to think and feel that there's no hope for ceasing violence and crime? Or, are you going to wait until it's one of your relatives or close friends become a victim of these two cancerous demonic monsters (violence and crime)?

People, just know that enough is enough of violence and crime and why continue to sit back and allow Satan to continue use human beings to increase violence and crime just like a wildfire that the firemen, politicians, pastors, etc. has no control over? It's going to take all of us, politicians, pastors, etc., to become knowledgeable about this book so that the information and strategies can be implemented successfully to conquer these two demonic spirits that have been unleashed by Satan decades ago and has gotten out of control. The law officers can't conquer the demons by themselves—they only apprehend and incarcerate the criminal and the system gains money (a fine). Needless to say, I often wonder if the legal system and the politics that are included, really have a heart and desire for violence and crime to cease. I don't really think so about *some* of the leaders because it's a money cliché and just think if violence and crime ceased, look at all of the positions and buildings that'll become obsolete, such as prisons, jailhouses, detention centers, attorneys, judges, prosecutors, jurors, etc. Now you see if this world was filled with genuine love instead of violence and crime, those positions will no longer be needed all because people have learned about the root solution in this book and they're no longer allowing Satan to control them. Instead, people are now having control over their own minds and actions, by learning how to love genuinely towards one another in every city, state, country, etc., globally. Stop for a moment and read this paragraph again until it clicks in your mind exactly why this God-given message (the root solution) in this book is being shared. Well, by now you should see that it's time to stop waiting, watching, blaming and pointing fingers as to who is responsible for violence and crime to cease and if you continue to wait on the politicians, mayors, etc. to implement a solution, crime and violence will never cease because it's going to take us (*everybody in all walks of life*) to implement the "Root Solution" that is shared in this book. Now, the Lord allowed me to share the answer to our cry regarding crime and violence, don't you think it's time to utilize it if we want to live in unity and share genuine love globally?

"The Root Solution—No More Bandages" Movement

I know you are in suspense and questions are roaming through your mind about a solution that has never been implemented—only bandaged. Well, allow me to cure your curiosity about this movement, which was placed on my heart by God almighty. This is a movement where people who have a passion for *violence and crime* to <u>cease</u> and will be highly supportive of the <u>root solution</u>, which is becoming better acquainted with God and Jesus, who is his son (although the Bible states that the father, son, and Holy Ghost are one), and participate in the movement by sharing and highly recommending the root solution, which is the book titled "God's Genuine Love—The Root Solution for Violence and Crime" to others.

The **"Root Solution-No More Bandages" Movement** for crime and violence stands up for only what it says, which means the <u>*main solution*</u> for violence and crime—no more temporary bandages. This movement also believes in making changes in the system to remove all bandages from the chaos and problems that the world (which means every state, country, continent, etc.) is experiencing and implement the "root solution". With sincerity, it's time for <u>everybody</u> on this earth to unite on one accord and become knowledgeable of the <u>root solution</u> and implement it, starting from the political offices on down to the citizens. People, there's no other solution, so let's stop bandaging the causes of violence and crime that for so many years the "so-called" solutions (better known as bandages) have failed.

When you become a supporter or a participant of the *Root Solution-No More Bandages* Movement, you are in agreement with the following statements:

1) You want violence and crime to cease in this world.

2) You want everybody to exemplify or pattern after God's

genuine Love.

3) You want everybody to share genuine love with one another meaning to do a deed from the heart—keeping in mind that you aren't trying to buy love, friendship, or family relationship but you are only doing a good deed because that's a pattern of God's Genuine Love. Didn't God go through the cities performing miracles and helping people such as the widow woman who was about to starve and the lame who couldn't walk? Didn't he also feed a multitude with two fishes and five loaves of bread? Wow! That illustrates his genuine love for all mankind and he wasn't helping people to buy their love or friendship. You just don't ever know if a person is struggling and has in mind to steal or rob to survive and you just might be the one to prevent a violent or criminal act by sharing a good deed and I can attest to that on numerous occasions.

4) You want any problem(s) whether it's a family, relationship, political, job, etc., to be resolved by starting from the *root* (meaning the motive, cause, misunderstanding, or lack of communication) of it—no bandaging (meaning trying to resolve the problem from the middle of it; lack of evidence; insufficient amount of information or concrete information).

5) You are in agreement and supportive of marches, parades, events, meetings, etc., to advocate for violence and crime to cease.

Lastly, the "Root Solution-No More Bandages" Movement informs the people that we have God-given power over the demonic tactics (violence and crime) that have been released from the pit of hell and Satan is the master of them, but the Lord stated in the Bible that one can put a 1,000 to flight and two can put 10,000 to flight— biblical chapters and verses (Leviticus. 26:8 and Deuteromy 32:30), *meaning everyone can have a positive* impact or help defeat those two demonic spirits that Satan utilizes through people's mind and action.

For decades, everybody has been wondering when and who will be victorious in conquering violence and crime, which today, is constantly spreading like a wildfire in the world. Well, it's time to stop sitting back expecting political officials (president, lawmakers, congress, police department, mayor, councilman, etc.) to conquer them alone—it's going to take every individual to play a role in conquering those two satanic forces and we must first obtain knowledge about how to approach them and this book that the Lord inspired me to write is the first step (which is preparation for war against Satan because God didn't give us the spirit of fear). So, starting today, start making preparation and no longer totally depend on higher authorities for the answer to violence and crime, because this book has the answer and strategies to defeat, decrease or even cease violence and crime. So now, what are you going to do with the answer or the "root solution?" All we have to do is adhere to this book, which is a second reference to the Bible—pray, and the Lord will fulfill his purpose for this book by conquering violence and crime. So, don't procrastinate, start exercising all what you have read in this book and let's be on a God's journey or mission to conquer violence and crime.

Satan and his elves have done enough damage in this world by using those two demonic forces (violence and crime) to end precious lives and possibly didn't have an opportunity to fulfill their spiritual mission that the Lord had planned for their lives. The Lord said that he has given us power to defeat whatever comes up against us and even power to move mountains, so don't you think it's about time for us to come together and do what the Lord said to do? He has given me the <u>root solution</u> along with all of the other weapons in this book to share with everyone and you know when God is the reign leader and we're the soldiers, we can tear Satan's violent and criminal kingdom down, which means introducing the knowledge in this book to others and implement the root solution along with the other valuable and beneficial knowledge that's shared in this book. That's how we will defeat and cease the two satanic forces that Satan instills in the minds of people to cause them to harm other innocent and precious beings.

Yes, it's time for a *change* and we're the ones who are responsible for making this change in life against violence and crime. So starting today, let's refocus and reprogram our minds and heart to say no more will I wait for someone else to provide, implement or tackle these two demonic spirits of violence and crime, I'm going to accept, implement and share the root solution given in this book to cease violence and crime. Just know that making this change to start loving genuinely isn't hard nor stressful because this is something that you must make up your mind to want and that is for violence and crime to cease and everybody live in unity and not division. Please know and remember that God gives us power over our thinking and thoughts and anything the mind conceives it can achieve, so let's start this journey and mission to cease violence and crime. People, we must start from somewhere and just know this mission isn't going to happen overnight but we'll start to see progress and crime rate decrease and as we keep implementing the root solution, the almighty God will cease crime and violence because he assigned me to reveal the root solution, so it's our job to start implementing and sharing it. When God gives an assignment don't you know he has a great purpose for the mission or assignment? So don't miss your blessing by not supporting what he wants his soldiers (you and me) to conquer and that's the demonic forces of violence and crime. Just know that King Jesus isn't sending us on this battlefield alone, so if you have love and compassion for yourself and others and want to stop seeing their lives being taken or assaulted—even people being victimized, take heed to the information shared in this book.

CHAPTER VII

SUMMARY OF THE BOOK

Now, that you have been well-educated about God's genuine love and how he shares it with all human beings; the attributes of God; your purpose for life; and the reasons or causes of people feeling unloved, are all topics that exemplifies what need to be accepted, exercised, embraced, and memorized in order to change the brutal thoughts and actions towards one another. Almighty God is our role model and it's imperative that all human beings follow his pattern of genuine love and *stop the violence, hate, malice, jealousy, envy, and criminal actions* toward our fellow brothers and sisters in this world.

Let's allow our love for one another be transformed into that genuine love so starting <u>today,</u> no more taking anger and frustration out on other innocent individuals by taking their lives, assaulting, bullying, snatching purses, hating, envy, robbing, stealing, burglary, arson, bombing, etc. You have spent your precious and valuable time and money to purchase and read this <u>life-changing</u> book, so don't let your time and money be spent in vain. Get all of the <u>*benefits*</u> that are shared in this book by allowing the knowledge you have attained about God's genuine love live in your hearts, minds, and inner beings. This world can be like heaven on earth, (an old saying), with the transformation of God's genuine love being shared throughout the world. So, let's start TODAY and fulfill the purpose for your lives that the Lord has ordained, and put a stop to crime and violence by utilizing genuine love. However, if you are not aware of the purpose (assignment or mission) for your life, just faithfully pray and ask our father what is the assignment he has ordained for your life because he had that purpose appointed before your birth. While waiting for your answer, be patient because he has his ways of revealing it. Next, accept your purpose with honor and fulfill it.

God chose my household and myself as the apples of his eyes and he has revealed several of my gifts and talents and some of them are the gift of intuition; the gift of discernment; the gift of healing and speaking blessings into my own life. The Lord's spiritual purpose for my life is to fulfill the answer to my life-long question to him and that is "What can I do to stop people from being violent and committing crimes because I'm tired of feeling the victim's pain and people becoming incarcerated criminals?" The answer is to share this book with the world and introduce the ***"Root Solution-No More Bandages"* Movement.**

When my son was about four or five years of age, the Lord spoke to me saying that the purpose for my son's life is to preach God's word and bring souls into his kingdom. Although my son has not fulfilled the purpose for his life yet, the Lord is still preparing him for his mission. People, don't just read this book then lay it aside, instead, *read* and *comprehend* what you are reading and accept the *benefits* that are shared with you in this ordained, and valuable book, so that it can make a positive and quick change in your lives. Use this book as a *reference* and a guide towards helping others to become knowledgeable about God's genuine love and ceasing the violence. In addition, recommend this reference to everyone you know and request that the shopping centers and grocery stores that you do business with make it available in their stores. Whether you know it or not, as a patron (library cardholder), you have the right to request books that interest you, to be carried in the library for checkout. Of course, dealing with the library system, you will probably have to request this book several times and have other people you know who has a library card to request "God's Genuine Love-The Root Solution for Violence and Crime", to be shared in the library for other patronages. By doing this, you are joining the movement in ceasing violence and crime, which is a great deed and the Lord will reward you for your contributing to help change lives, save lives, and make a difference in the lives of others in this world.

Allow this valuable book to become your second biblical reference because the Bible is always first in our lives and just know that the information shared in this book isn't temporary or a bandage – it's concrete and the main, or one and (only one), solution for violence and crime, so don't ever feel that over time "God's Genuine Love – The Root Solution for Violence and Crime" has become obsolete or is no longer beneficial because the information in the Bible will never become obsolete and the Bible has been in existence since the beginning of earth, so always have both of these books with you at all times and continue to meditate on all of the scriptures given in this life-changing book.

-SAY NO TO *CRIME* AND *STOP* THE VIOLENCE-

Author Ruby Mack

I was born in Jackson, MS where I currently resides and I'm a single parent who reared two children. I also completed my education in Mississippi and attended Brown Elementary, Rowan Jr. High and Lanier High School (Class of 1983). I also earned an Associate Degree in Business Management Technology from Hinds Community College in 1997, and a Bachelor's Degree in Business Administration from Mississippi College in Clinton, MS. I enjoy singing, dancing, crocheting, skating, playing basketball, cooking, writing; but most of all, I enjoy attending church, sharing Christ, inspiring and motivating others. The Lord placed it on my heart to write this book titled, "God's Genuine Love-The Root Solution for Violence and Crime", because of the love, compassion, and empathy I have for the people in this world (known and unknown). I'm confident that this book will make a <u>positive change</u> in the world by

teaching the readers the true meaning of love; how to love yourself and others; their purpose for life on Earth; and most importantly, how to avoid and cease violence and crime. Another upcoming book soon to be published will most definitely assist people who are still mourning the death of someone who is dear to them and don't know how to cope with it. In addition, it will also help readers to understand death and last, but not least, how to accept the Lord's work when death visits. I empathize with people and deeply feel their pains, heartaches and griefs.

Choose **TODAY**, *to partner with Author Ruby Mack to inspire and share with the world, "There's hope for violence and crime to cease" and together, we can accomplish this God-given mission. Join the "Root Solution-No More Bandages" Movement—against violence and crime. Together, we can send the two satanic forces (violence and crime) back to the pit of hell where they were released.*

I love you passionately.

www.ingramcontent.com/pod-product-compliance
Lightning Source LLC
Chambersburg PA
CBHW071405290426
44108CB00014B/1688